Flimflam Man

The Tragedy of Barack Hussein Obama

Monty Pelerin

Flimflam Man
The Tragedy of Barack Hussein Obama

Monty Pelerin

This book is for sale at http://leanpub.com/flimflamman

This version was published on 2014-06-17

This book owes its pedigree to many intellectual influences. There are too many to list, but a few are especially important. Free market economics provided the basis for economic and political views. Ludwig von Mises, Friedrich Hayek, Milton Friedman and James Buchanan were important influences. Political cynics like H. L. Mencken and Albert J. Nock were also important.

The book owes its existence to my wife, Joan, who has put up with my long hours on the computer and made me a better person.

The book owes its improvements to readers who offer suggestions and commentary. Keep the reviews coming, they are very helpful. The book is updated with many of your suggestions and corrections.

Contents

Introduction

The Website

Monty Pelerin's World[1] is a website which began in September of 2009. It deals with economic, political and financial issues. You may email Monty Pelerin at montypelerin@gmail.com or contact him through the website. Feedback is always appreciated.

What began as a hobby turned into a greater commitment. The country contained too much folly passing for wisdom, news and analysis to deal with part time. The website became a full-time effort, now containing 4,200 posts.

Flimflam Man

This book deals with President Barack Obama and his phenomenal fall from grace. Obama entered office more popular than John F. Kennedy or anyone else in modern history. His performance suggests he will leave rated below the hapless Jimmy Carter, generally acknowledged to be the worst president of the last several generations.

With about two and a half years left in his second term, the bottom still is not in sight for Obama. His policies have failed and he has become an embarrassment for America. The economy hasn't recovered despite unprecedented programs that will only impoverish future generations. Foreign policy is disastrous. Allies are nervous and no longer trust the US. Enemies are emboldened. The world has become a much more dangerous place.

---

[1]http://www.economicnoise.com

Obama supporters in the Democrat Party and the media have reason to worry. Their man has not lived up to expectations which threatens to discredit them. None of this should be surprising as there was nothing in Obama's resume to suggest he could handle the job of President of the United States of America. Peter Wehner of Commentary[2] magazine commented on Obama's problem:

> We've learned the hard way that Mr. Obama's skill sets are far more oriented toward community organizing than they are to governing. On every front, he is over matched by events. It's painful to watch a man who is so obviously in over his head.

This problem came with the man. This outcome was entirely foreseeable based on Obama's limited background and experience.

The Developing Problem

Once the imagery and adulation wore off, people began to see the shortcomings. This Wizard of Oz was not some bumbling, harmless old man. He was pompous, arrogant, mean, disingenuous and incompetent.

The Democrat superstar is now a political liability. The media and the Democrat Party have serious issues with his failure. Both promoted him and both will be affected by his failure. 2014 mid-term election polling suggests that massive political change may be coming. Republicans are expected to add to their majority in the House and re-take the Senate.

The extraordinary number of alleged scandals, several of which have the potential to sink Obama's presidency, make the decision to stand by him especially risky. The number identified in this book is

---

[2]//www.commentarymagazine.com/2014/05/21/the-new-obama-narrative-epic-incompetence/

24. However, the recent emergence of the Veterans Administration disgrace and the Bowe Bergdahl prisoner exchange move that up to 26. The two recent ones were uncovered as the book went to print.

An Unlikely But Possible Ending

Impeachment is a harsh word and an extraordinary event. Its likelihood is not yet high, although Obama's situation is trending toward the precarious. No one knows what may be uncovered if real, honest investigations commence. Benghazi seems to be an obvious cover-up. The IRS scandal concerns most Americans and both sides of Congress. Alone, these two are likely more serious than what led to problems for Richard Nixon. Other vulnerabilities beyond these exist.

If Obama becomes too big a liability Democrats and supporting media may be forced to make a serious choice – stand by him or protect themselves. Obama's precarious position now endangers that of his supporters. At his rate of decline, these supporters may consider it a wise strategy to abandon him.

There is little if any loyalty in politics. Obama and his Chicago outsiders have accrued less than most politicians. They are outsiders and have little use for Congress or normal channels. Their arrogance has not pleased the old bulls of Congress. There is no store of good will that protects this Administration.

At some point Obama could become too big a drag on his supporters. They must feed their families after he is gone. If that possibility is threatened, then Obama is in trouble. Obama then, at least figuratively, *becomes worth more dead than alive.* That is, his supporters are in better shape without him than with him. If that point is reached, supporters will turn on him like piranhas. Politics is not noble. It is a dirty business. Survival is all that matters. Loyalty and ethics get only lip service.

Many of the chapters in this book originally appeared on Monty

Pelerin's website. Some also appeared elsewhere, on sites like American Thinker, PJ Media and Zerohedge. The articles have been mostly rewritten with the intent to improve their readability. The prescience, or lack thereof, was intended to be maintained.

Political Disclaimer

This book deals with Barack Obama's presidency which began approximately eight months prior to the first website post. It is not incorrect to assume that the election of Barack Obama and his approach to economics and governance motivated the website.

It would be incorrect to infer that the author is a Republican or is active in politics. Were the website to have begun earlier, it would have been critical of George W. Bush. One of the earliest posts was a retrospective one, questioning whether George W. Bush was the worst president.

H. L. Mencken captures my attitude regarding politics and govern-ment:

> Every decent man is ashamed of the government he lives under.

Those who are familiar with Mencken know there are hundreds of statements that could have been selected to convey his disdain for politics and politicians. This one was chosen not because it was the best, but because it was convenient and brief.

A bias is reflected in the book. It is not one that discriminates between Democrats or Republicans. It reflects Mencken's attitude regarding government. Government has a legitimate role in society, but that role is extremely limited.

That is my bias. It is not with respect to Democrats or Republicans. I am an equal-opportunity disliker of both.

The Myth of Government

Statism, which is what exists today, is not governance. It is plunder. Statists dominate both political parties. Both support the myth of government, which is that government is a force for good and can improve society.

Government does no good that couldn't be done better without it. It is capable of doing great harm, even when its intentions are good. That is why it is best kept small and limited. Statism is the source of most of our current problems, whether they be labeled economic, political or societal.

Believing government is a solution to problems is akin to providing a fox to protect your chickens. Government creates problems. More government makes these problems worse. Expecting government to fix problems they created is like expecting more heroin to help the drug addict. Bigger government only means bigger problems and bigger hangovers.

Organization of The Book

The book is generally presented in chronological order. It could be considered a summary diary because much of it is drawn from Monty Pelerin's World[3]. This website is still active and contains contemporaneous reactions to events as they happened.

Most chapters provide the date of the original post. Time gaps between chapters can be filled by referring to the website, although the book was intended to stand on its own.

Sections of The Book

The book is divided into these sections:

---

[3]http://www.economicnoise.com

Each section deals with different time periods in the Obama Presidency.

The period ahead is going to be exciting. Historians of the future will view this time as an important inflection point in American history. The country can either return to its founding principles or it can continue its journey toward serfdom.

The remaining two and a half years of the Obama presidency will be contentious. An ideologue president will attempt to further impose Socialism on what once was the bastion of freedom. The political battle will be mostly show. Few politicians from either party care about principles. They care about power and retaining it.

Politicians from both sides of the aisle are generally in agreement with his direction. Many disagree over the speed with which he wants to move.

The Tea Party, hardly an organized party, is a threat to both sides of the establishment. It represents pushback on that part of the public which recognizes what is going on.

Hang on, the remainder of Obama's term could be more exciting than that already seen. Historians of the future are apt to view this time as an important inflection point in American history.

Rev 3.1

I MESSIAH TO FLIMFLAM MAN

How It Began

During the Democrat primaries, concerns regarding Barack Obama surfaced. Large gaps in his past, no known friends or associates and no real experience raised warning flags for those who were looking. The media chose to ignore these shortcomings and promoted the Messiah euphoria or what was called "Obamamania."

There was nothing, **absolutely nothing**, in Barack Obama's background to suggest he had the capability to perform as President of the United States.

Nevertheless, he was a perfect candidate. Hollywood could not have cast the role any better. Obama was the perfect lead in a presidential movie. His appearance and manner were impeccable. Hollywood actors had to be jealous of his thespian talents.

The media supported his campaign and protected him. Obama was marketed perfectly by David Axelrod. He knocked out the heavily-favored Hillary Clinton and the feared Clinton machine to gain the nomination.

His or Hillary's election was virtually assured given the Bush fatigue and the shop-worn and ineffective opponent, John McCain.

Obama's Arrival

The conditions Obama encountered upon entering office in January of 2009 were numerous and serious. Early problems included the following:

- The country was in a terrible economic and financial crisis.
- The government's response to the financial crisis angered many citizens.
- The health care debacle did not exist, but was quickly created.
- Political unrest was unlikely to subside because the economic problems could drag on for years.
- There was risk of civil unrest.
- Washington was viewed as arrogant and out of touch.
- Many believed Washington and the financial industry to be an oligarchy, running the country while looking out only for themselves.

The country had suffered a financial crisis so severe that it might properly have been called a Depression. Unprecedented, and some argued unconstitutional, steps were taken to bail out major financial institutions and re-start the economy.

The recession was declared over in June 2009, a claim that seemed incredible then and more so in hindsight. Federal Reserve "quantitative easing" continues today, as does the use of the word "recovering" when discussing the economy. It is five years since the recession was declared officially over. George Orwell must have been the economist who made the call.

The issues inherited by Obama are no better today than they were five and a half years ago. Arguably some were made worse, most notably the self-inflicted wound known as ObamaCare.

1 The Legend Of Bagger Obama

JANUARY 5, 2010

> This post is chronologically out of order, but only slightly. It is first because it provides a description of the arrival of Barack Obama. For those who tend to skip around, the chapter entitled "President Quixote's Legacy," which can be found near the beginning of Part Two, provides insight into Obama's mindset. Understanding what apparently motivates him might be useful in judging the policies and actions he adopted.

It is 2008. An unknown figure steps from the mist. No one knows his background. There is no birth certificate. No college transcripts or other records. No known friends. No apparent experience. A virtual blank slate stares at you. Are you watching a remake of the eponymous "Legend of Bagger Vance?" No, you are witnessing the emergence of Barack Obama on his march to power.

1.1 Bagger Vance

"The Legend of Bagger Vance" was a Robert Redford directed movie made in 2000. The principal actors were Will Smith, Matt Damon, Charlize Theron and Jack Lemmon (his last movie). The film was about a fictional golf event in 1931, held in Georgia. Smith played the central role of Bagger Vance, a mystical and mysterious caddy.

Damon played Rannulph Junuh, whose life, golf game and love interest Bagger magically rejuvenated. The story was set against an epic golf match Junuh played against Walter Hagen and Bobby Jones.

Awesomestories.com[1] provided the following background for the film:

> As Steven Pressfield[2] (author of The Legend of Bagger Vance[3]) has acknowledged, Bagger Vance, and the story of his legend, are based on the Hindu epic and scriptural poem, the *Bhagavad-Gita*[4]. In the epic, Bhagavan is the "Supreme Personality" who helps his follower, Arjuna, understand much about war and about life.

In a review of the film[5], the following observations were offered:

> ... co-producer Michael Nozik described Bagger as a "Native American coyote trickster," and costar [Charlize] Theron has expressed her fascination with how "you don't ever know where he comes from or where he's going."

1.2 Bagger Obama

The Legend of Bagger Obama started with a masterfully crafted and executed presidential campaign. It was a campaign of personality, centered on a young, unknown, but messianic figure. The Clinton

---

[1]http://www.awesomestories.com/religion/bagger-vance/who-is-bagger-vance
[2]http://www.stevenpressfield.com/
[3]http://www.awesomestories.com/assets/the-legend-of-bagger-vance
[4]http://www.theosociety.org/pasadena/gita/bg-eg-hp.htm
[5]http://www.nicksflickpicks.com/bagvance.html

machine, the most feared force in politics, was taken out first. Then an inept Senator McCain was easily defeated.

Visions of Camelot redux filled the media. Millions supported the shadowy and charismatic man. A groundswell of popular support, hope and goodwill ushered him into office. Marvin Olasky[6] reported on some of the reactions:

> Tom Brokaw compared Obama's inauguration to the overthrow of Communism in 1989: "I was in Prague when that happened. . . . The streets were filled with joy." *CBS Early Show* co-anchor Maggie Rodriguez rhapsodized, "A new day is dawning here in the nation's capital. . . . Does it get any better, or more beautiful, or more spectacular, than this?"

The International community was equally infatuated. Obama was awarded the Nobel Peace Prize based on nothing more than imagery and expectations.

The trappings of office added additional majesty to his persona. Obama was a rock star. His presence dominated the airwaves and newspapers. Exaggerations (or lies) became truth if he uttered them.

This "Supreme Personality" believed his mere presence and pronouncements constituted governance. Management and decision-making seemed beneath him.

It was as if Bagger Vance, himself, had ascended to the White House. It was just how Bagger might govern. Mere pronouncements, filled with mystical wisdom, would solve the world's problems. Presence and image would replace decision-making. That was what Bagger knew and did.

---

[6] http://townhall.com/columnists/MarvinOlasky/2010/01/05/after_the_swoon

1.3 Reality Versus Movies

Movies are easier to script than real-life. Bagger Obama's "legend" soon began to falter. A teleprompter malfunction exposed oratory skills no better than those of his ridiculed, "illiterate" predecessor. Campaign promises were quickly abandoned. Embarrassments abroad developed, as did a conspicuous pattern of waffling on issues.

Unlike a movie, real-life has angles never intended to be filmed. Campaigns can be carefully staged and orchestrated. After election, all camera angles come into play. Staging can still be attempted, but not as effectively.

The young emperor soon began to be viewed as without clothes and without crown. Some of his biggest supporters in the media began criticizing, even satirizing Bagger. From Marvin Olasky:

> Jon Stewart's *The Daily Show* on Comedy Central is often a leading indicator of sentiment among younger voters. Stewart last month waxed sarcastic regarding not only Democratic spending and deficit-creation, but also about Obama's personal style of implying frankness and then serving up bromides.

> Maureen Dowd's *New York Times* column is often a leading indicator of sentiment among older liberal voters. She wrote recently, "The animating spirit that electrified his political movement has sputtered out. If we could see a Reduced Shakespeare summary of Obama's presidency so far, it would read: Dither, dither, speech. Foreign trip, bow, reassure. Seminar, summit. Shoot a jump shot with the guys, throw out the first pitch in mom jeans. Compromise, concede, close the deal. Dither, dither, water down, news conference."

Stripped of his protective aura, Bagger Obama was reduced to an ordinary man, subject to the usual judgment and scrutiny. He was seen as just another politician. "The One" had morphed into "Just Another One" (ordinary politician that is, with all the accompanying baggage).

1.4 Reality Always Rules

Ayn Rand stated that you can avoid reality but reality is not going to avoid you. That observation seems beyond Obama's comprehension.

Sans halo, Bagger Obama's campaign phrases seemed sophomoric and hackneyed. "Yes we can!" had no meaning. "Hope and Change," conveniently imprecise and effective in a campaign, was useless for governing. The public passed judgment now in terms of effectiveness rather than awe. Warts and blemishes were apparent once the Messiah lens was removed.

The prolonged Afghanistan troop decision, scripted as the measured consideration of a wise leader, did not play well. It was seen merely as another example of a politician stalling while searching for a political strategy. The "correct" war of the campaign became a political problem. Geopolitics or troop safety seemed secondary to political considerations.

The Guantanamo (Gitmo) base closing represented another failed campaign promise. The decision was postponed for more than a year. The base may never be closed. Attempts to transfer prisoners to other places were clumsy and replete with political bribes.

Health-care reform morphed through endless iterations of disjointed efforts. At the end, there was no discernible logic behind the plan. Inconsistencies, deals, falsified data and outright lies were evident to anyone willing to pay attention. Despite the problems and unpopularity, health care was pushed forward. Congressional

Democrats sacrificed the best health care system in the world and the American taxpayer with their passage of the Affordable Care Act.

Nowhere was the lack of leadership more apparent than in the economic sphere. Promises and forecasts were consistently wrong. The vaunted stimulus package was little more than large-scale looting, cronyism and vote-buying. Increasingly, non-government economists agreed that economic policies were harmful.

In response, the Administration maintained that a recovery was under way. But citizens knew that stock prices were lower than they were in 1999, no net job creation occurred this century and fore-closures and bankruptcies were increasing. No alternative, credible plan was offered.

The real Bagger Vance rehabilitated Junah's golf game to the point where Junah competed with Hagen and Jones. His magic was "real" in the fictional sense that he mystically shaped outcomes and events.

Bagger Obama strode onto the stage selling the same magic. His "magic" was to have been fixing our economy and geopolitical role. Since his arrival, conditions in both areas worsened. This Bagger's magic was "pretend" and did not work, at least outside of his own mind.

Obama sold a product he could not deliver. Image and reality collided. Reality always wins such contests.

The unfolding tragedy is that everyone but Bagger Obama seems to recognize what happened. What was once viewed by people as confidence, control and wisdom is now seen as narcissism, naiveté and self-absorption. Yet, Bagger Obama continues playing his role, seemingly oblivious to the changing views of his followers.

1.5 Danger Point For Obama

We are at a dangerous point in both the Presidency of Barack Obama and the country. Does the Administration have any idea of what to do? Do they believe they can continue to use Hollywood imagery in lieu of real, hard decisions? Hype, rhetoric and Greek columns are now irrelevant. Markets and enemies are immune to such dramaturgy.

For Bagger Obama, it is difficult to visualize how this ends. **It is unlikely that he can rehabilitate his presidency, because there is no way to rehabilitate the phony image.** A different image will not work. People will not fall for another marketing ruse.

Americans are forgiving people, but they have never been kind to con men. The most likely scenario is that Bagger Obama is a one-term embarrassment to the country, the world and the Democrat party.

Obama's fiction was great, but short-lived. He was a wonderful actor, able to effectively play a President on TV, for a while. All form and no substance works for a movie but not real life with real problems, decisions and adversaries. The Fall sweeps have come and gone. The Obama show did not pass muster. Unlike TV, mercilessly this show cannot be canceled for three more years.

Somewhere from beyond the mist the real Bagger Vance must be chuckling as he watches his wannabe copycat. Perhaps he would provide the following advice to Obama:

> "You know you can just go ahead and creep off somewhere I'll tell folk you took sick... Truth be told, ain't nobody gonna really object... In fact, they'd probably be happy as bugs in a bake shop to see you pack up and go home..."

For Bagger Vance this may be humorous. For most of us, however, the next three years will seem like a dangerous eternity.

2 Is Obama Failing Along With Everything Else?

SEPTEMBER 29, 2009

The country is not in good shape. The economy has not recovered. Nor will it, given the economic and political policies in place and proposed. Foreign policy is disoriented, with no discernible theme or coherence.

Barack Obama is ultimately responsible for domestic and foreign policy. While early in his tenure, it is reasonable to say that his policies are not helping. They are making matters worse.

2.1 The Economy

The US economy is in the worst shape it has been in since the 1930s. The financial system still borders on collapse with no apparent remedies for financial system weaknesses. Additional taxpayer and Federal Reserve subsidies will be required.

The Federal government is itself hopelessly insolvent, destined to eventually default on some or many of its debts and social commitments. Some states and local governments are in even worse condition.

The international currency system is unsustainable. The dollar as a world currency is not forever, but it is difficult to see what might replace it near-term. Change in currency regimes is always destabilizing. Devastating effects on the country that loses its preferred status occur and ripple through to other world economies.

In light of all this, financial markets appear overvalued. However, the Federal Reserve is engaged in a "great experiment" to determine whether they can "print" their way out of financial crisis. The effects on financial assets of this inflation may drive markets higher and create more economic and financial distortions or bubbles. The Fed suggested as much when explaining what they hoped to achieve.

The economy is not in good shape. Government engages in chicanery to convince people otherwise.

Whether they succeed or not is almost irrelevant. Success via these means will be superficial and temporary. **The bubbles blown today become tomorrow's crises.**

2.2 Foreign Policy

Like the economy, geopolitical problems might be likened to those of the 1930's. Iran openly defies the United States and the world community by continuing its pursuit of nuclear weapons. Its leader appears half-crazed, driven by an apocalyptic vision. Israel believes its very existence is threatened and probably will act if no one else stops Iran.

Russia is reasserting itself. North Korea is still a disoriented nuclear power that behaves like a child demanding attention. Chavez is creating problems in South America. China has its head down for the moment, concentrating on economic development. And the US appears to be in another Vietnam-type quagmire with Afghanistan.

Obama seems to think that "playing nice" with bad actors will get results.

2.3 The Presidency

If the economic and geo-political issues were not enough, the beginnings of another, rather astonishing, collapse of a President may be underway.

Obama's economic policy (arguably incorrect) will fail. Failed programs, while necessary for a failed Presidency, are not sufficient. At this point, it is premature to make the claim that Obama has failed. Yet, as time passes, the evidence tilts steadily in this direction.

A President fails when public opinion turns against him. Trends in polls suggest that may be happening, but polls and people are fickle. A better indicator might be the reactions of supporters.

Some of President Obama's strongest supporters were in the media, so many in fact that the opposition complained about media bias. These complaints continue, asserting that the press treats his administration with kid gloves and slants or does not report negative news.

Political assessments from media supporters may be turning. One example is presented below where Rick Moran[1] , cites well-known liberal columnist Richard Cohen of the NY Times. Whether this article is a sign of a turn in press behavior is moot.

Richard Cohen waiting for Obama to realize he's president

September 29, 2009

by Rick Moran

Richard Cohen,[2] writing in the Washington Post, has finally noticed the same thing we here at AT have noted many times previously; Barack Obama is not leading as chief executive but is still stuck in campaign mode as if he is still running for the office:

---

[1]http://www.americanthinker.com/website/2009/09/roger_cohen_waiting_for_obama. html

[2]http://www.washingtonpost.com/wp-dyn/content/article/2009/09/28/ AR2009092802484.html

The trouble with Obama is that he gets into the moment and means what he says for that moment only. He meant what he said when he called Afghanistan a "war of necessity[3]" and now is not necessarily so sure. He meant what he said about the public option in his health-care plan and then again maybe not[4]. He would not prosecute[5] CIA agents for getting rough with detainees and then again maybe he would.

Most tellingly, he gave Congress an August deadline for passage of health-care legislation "Now, if there are no deadlines, nothing gets done in this town . . . " and then let it pass. It seemed not to occur to Obama that a deadline comes with a consequence meet it or else.

Obama lost credibility with his deadline-that-never-was, and now he threatens to lose some more with his posturing toward Iran. He has gotten into a demeaning dialog with Ahmadinejad, an accomplished liar. (The next day, the Iranian used a news conference to counter Obama and, days later, Iran tested some intermediate-range missiles.) Obama is our version of a Supreme Leader, not given to making idle threats,

[3]http://www.washingtonpost.com/wp-dyn/content/article/2009/08/17/AR2009081701657.html

[4]http://www.washingtonpost.com/wp-dyn/content/article/2009/09/09/AR2009090901771.html

[5]http://www.washingtonpost.com/wp-dyn/content/article/2009/04/16/AR2009041602768.html

setting idle deadlines, reversing course on momentous issues, creating a TV crisis where none existed or, unbelievably, pitching Chicago[6] for the 2016 Olympics. Obama's the president. Time he understood that.

These comments from Cohen in the NY Times are a big deal. They recognize Obama weaknesses and they come from a liberal institution and respected writer. Moran adds his take:

> ... this is what we get when America elects someone with zero experience doing anything except running for higher office. If all someone has done of note is run a campaign, you are likely to get a president who sees the job as nothing more than an extension of his previous efforts to get elected.

> I think it should be obvious that the fallacy "Presidents always grow into the job" should be debunked once and for all. Presidents bring to the job the skill set, the moral compass, the abilities they have shown previously in their lives. They don't suddenly learn to become a "leader." If they have not demonstrated that capability by the time they are Obama's age, they never will.

Mr. Moran and Mr. Cohen identified some of the problems with Barack Obama. These will plague him throughout his presidency.

[6]http://www.washingtonpost.com/wp-dyn/content/article/2009/09/28/AR2009092801150.html

3 America, The Ego Has Landed

OCTOBER 2, 2009

To paraphrase Houston Command Central: "America, The Ego Has Landed." And not smoothly.

3.1 The Olympic Embarrassment

Today's Copenhagen announcement was a political disaster heard around the world. It raised more issues concerning the image and competency of President Obama. Regardless of one's politics, another failed Presidency is not good for the country. Given the current geopolitical and economic situation, it could be especially dangerous as discussed earlier[1].

Unfortunately the Copenhagen fiasco, along with a disastrous job report today, provide more evidence of a failing Presidency.

A harsh political evaluation was offered by the American Thinker (a conservative website):

3.2 American Thinker Reacts

Chicago out of Olympics consideration (updated)

Thomas Lifson

---

[1]http://www.economicnoise.com/?p=350

Dude, where's my charisma?

In a huge slap in the face for Barack, Michelle, and the Oprah, Chicago was the first city eliminated from Olympic consideration.

It turns out the world is getting sick of Mr. Know It All. The President of France openly mocks him[2], and now the Olympic Committee is unimpressed with his wonderfulness.

He is having even a worse day than David Letterman. He made it all about himself. Ben Smith of Politico wrote[3] before the decision:

Obama's pitch to the International Olympic Committee this morning is very much about his and America's identity, and not the IOC's sometimes transactional politics, raising the stakes for the decision:

> We stand at a moment in history when the fate of each nation is inextricably linked to the fate of all nations " a time of common challenges that require common effort. And I ran for President because I believed deeply that at this defining moment, the United States of America has a responsibility to help in that effort, to forge new partnerships with the nations and the peoples of the world".

---

[2]http://www.ocregister.com/articles/obama-world-president-2589546-sarkozy-russia
[3]http://www.politico.com/websites/bensmith/1009/Obamas_pitch_in_Copenhagen.html

Richard Baehr adds:

> It would be hard to exaggerate how hu-
> miliating is the IOC vote with Chicago go-
> ing out in the first round, with the lowest
> score of the 4 cites. So much for the theory
> that the world loves America more under
> Obama.This is a huge embarrassment for
> Obama, given he showed up for the pre-
> sentation. Obviously, he neither can count,
> or control votes on the IOC, the way he
> may in the Congress. This will not help
> him with any part of his domestic agenda.
> A key part of his message has been that
> he is not Bush, and presents a different
> America to the world. Andrew Young won
> the 1996 games for Atlanta during the first
> Bush presidency. Obama could not do it for
> Chicago.

Ed Lasky adds:

> He has done zero since elected " except
> cause some damage internationally.
> Stimulus bill was cooked by Congress, not
> him. Health Care: stalled; Card Check: stalled;
> Cap andTrade[4]: stalled.
> He has empowered unions and the left wing-
> which is causing businesses to postpone
> investment[5] and hiring. I have a radiologist

[4]http://www.americanthinker.com/website/2009/10/chicago_out_of_olympics_consid.
html
[5]http://www.americanthinker.com/website/2009/10/chicago_out_of_olympics_consid.
html

friend who told me his practice and the hos-
pital re postponing purchase of equipment
because they have no idea how much they
will earn in the future.

4 A Failed Presidency

NOVEMBER 19, 2009

Over the past few months the risks of a Failed Presidency have become apparent. No one should want this outcome, regardless of party affiliation. It is harmful to the economy, the country and the world. Yet that appears to be where we are headed.

Seth Leibsohn, in *National Review*, summarized it this way:

> "This is reminiscent of the Jimmy Carter years — the last time the U.S. was seen as weak — unable to move and coax other countries, unable to reassure dependent allies, unable to have the respect of the world and, of course, unable to move the mullocracy of Iran."

Even the liberal media are questioning the effectiveness of the President. The media, which would like to be in full Camelot mode, has been slow to react and lags behind what many recognized months ago. Yet, quotes like these, suggest the media may be catching up:

The New York Times reports:

> "China held firm against most American demands. With China's micro-management of Mr. Obama's appearances in the country, the trip did more to showcase China's ability to push back against outside pressure than it did to advance the main issues on Mr. Obama's agenda, analysts said."

The Washington Post:

> "If there was any significant change during this trip, in fact, it was in the United States' newly conciliatory and sometimes laudatory tone. . . . Obama's trip stood in stark contrast to visits by his predecessors."

The New York Times stated that Obama was given "less respect than was given presidents Bush or Clinton." The above quotes are found in the article by Leibsohn who concluded:

> "Not a very good first year for America, or the world, under a new leadership that promised a new respect, a new start, and a new way of doing business. It's new alright — it just isn't any good."

The president has failed, probably irretrievably so. The dream cannot be rebuilt because there was never a foundation beneath it. It was all show and no substance. Yes, it created excitement and (false) hope. But so did Elmer Gantry and James Jones.

There never was any substance to the man or his Administration. The image was like an old Hollywood set, all facade and no depth. Now the winds of reality are slowly and inexorably tearing away the facade.

Politicians in Congress see these signs and read the polls. At this point they are trying to decide whether Obama and his Administration can regain their footing. If not, then the politicians will begin to protect themselves against threats to their own careers. For the Republicans that probably means pouring gasoline on ship Obama. For the Democrats, it is a more difficult problem. Ultimately, I believe they will abandon the rotting ship.

Politicians in both parties are like rats; they are survivors. All politicians take the course which provides them the best chance for individual survival. Loyalty be damned.

Hang on, this will be a rough period ahead.

5 President of The World Losing Support There Also

DECEMBER 1, 2009

> *"Not only are things not getting fixed, they may be getting more broken."*

Peter Wehner describes how the world is reacting to Barack Obama. These excerpts provide a couple of judgments (the full article is shown below):

> It's "amateur hour at the White House," according to Leslie Gelb[1], president emeritus of the Council on Foreign Relations and a former official in the Carter administration.

> "Not only are things not getting fixed, they may be getting more broken," according to Michael Hirsh at Newsweek. When even such strong Obama supporters as Gelb and Hirsh reach these conclusions, you know things must be unraveling.

These comments are hugely important. Both gentlemen are knowledgeable supporters of the liberal agenda. That they recognize and are willing to speak out on these problems is very significant. One ounce of supporter criticism is worth 100 pounds of polling data.

Here is the entire article:

---

[1] http://www.thedailybeast.com/websites-and-stories/2009-11-22/think-before-you-travel

The Unmasking of Barack Obama

Peter Wehner[2] 11.30.2009

The overseas reviews for President Obama's foreign policy are starting to pour in " and they're not favorable. Bob Ainsworth, the British defense secretary, has blamed Obama for the decline in British public support for the war in Afghanistan. According to the *Telegraph*[3]:

> Mr. Ainsworth took the unprecedented step of publicly criticizing the U.S. President and his delays in sending more troops to bolster the mission against the Taliban. A "period of hiatus" in Washington " and a lack of clear direction " had made it harder for ministers to persuade the British public to go on backing the Afghan mission in the face of a rising death toll, he said. Senior British Government sources have become increasingly frustrated with Mr. Obama's "dithering" on Afghanistan, the *Daily Telegraph* disclosed earlier this month, with several former British defense chiefs echoing the concerns.

The President is "Obama the Impotent," according to Steven Hill[4] of the *Guardian*. The *Economist* calls Obama[5] the "Pacific (and pussyfooting) president." The

---

[2]http://www.commentarymagazine.com/websites/index.php/category/contentions?author_name=wehner

[3]http://www.telegraph.co.uk/news/newstopics/politics/defence/6646179/Bob-Ainsworth-criticises-Barack-Obama-over-Afghanistan.html

[4]http://www.guardian.co.uk/commentisfree/cifamerica/2009/sep/22/obama-un-climate-change-europe

[5]http://www.economist.com/opinion/displaystory.cfm?story_id=14915118

Financial Times[6] refers to "relations between the U.S. and Europe, which started the year of talks as allies, near breakdown." The German magazine *Der Spiegel*[7] accuses the president of being "dishonest with Europe" on the subject of climate change. Another withering piece in Der Spiegel[8]_, titled "Obama's Nice Guy Act Gets Him Nowhere on the World Stage," lists the instances in which Obama is being rolled. The *Jerusalem Post*[9] puts it this way: "Everybody is saying no to the American president these days. And it's not just that they're saying no, it's also the way they're saying no." "He talks too much," a Saudi academic[10] who had once been smitten with Barack Obama tells the Middle East scholar Fouad Ajami. The Saudi "has wearied of Mr. Obama and now does not bother with the Obama oratory," according to Ajami. But "he is hardly alone, this academic. In the endless chatter of this region, and in the commentaries offered by the press, the theme is one of disappointment. In the Arab-Islamic world, Barack Obama has come down to earth."

Indeed he has, and only Obama and his increasingly clueless administration seem unaware of this.

On almost every front, progress is nonexistent. In many instances, things are getting worse rather than better. The enormous goodwill that Obama's election was met with hasn't been leveraged into anything useful and tangible. Rather, our allies are now questioning

---

[6]http://www.ft.com/cms/s/0/e4328854-a6da-11de-bd14-00144feabdc0.html?nclick_check=1

[7]http://www.spiegel.de/international/world/0,1518,661678,00.html

[8]http://www.spiegel.de/international/world/0,1518,662822,00.html

[9]http://www.jpost.com/servlet/Satellite?cid=1253198168048&pagename=JPArticle%2FShowFull

[10]http://online.wsj.com/article/SB10001424052748703499404574558300500152682.html

America's will, while our adversaries are becoming increasingly emboldened. The United States looks weak and uncertain. It's "amateur hour at the White House," according to Leslie Gelb[11], president emeritus of the Council on Foreign Relations and a former official in the Carter administration. "Not only are things not getting fixed, they may be getting more broken," according to Michael Hirsh[12] at *Newsweek*. When such strong Obama supporters as Gelb and Hirsh reach these conclusions, you know things must be unraveling.

It's no mystery as to why. President Obama's approach to international relations is simplistic and misguided. It is premised on the belief that American concessions to our adversaries will beget goodwill and concessions in return; that American self-abasement is justified; that the American decline is inevitable (and in some respects welcome); and that diplomacy and multilateralism are ends rather than means to an end.

Right now the overwhelming issue on the public's mind is the economy, where Obama is also having serious problems. But national-security issues matter a great deal, and they remain the unique responsibility of the president. With every passing month, Barack Obama looks more and more like his Democratic predecessor Jimmy Carter: irresolute, unsteady, and over matched. The president and members of his own party will find out soon enough, though, that Obama the Impotent isn't what they had in mind when they elected him. We are witnessing the unmasking, and perhaps the unmaking, of Barack Obama.

---

[11]http://www.thedailybeast.com/websites-and-stories/2009-11-22/think-before-you-travel

[12]http://www.newsweek.com/id/224190

6 Health Care Vaporizes Obama Presidency

JANUARY 27, 2010

> *If there is one thing that will be pointed to as the turning point of the Obama Presidency, it will be the passage of ObamaCare. The implementation of this bill made it possible for even the most ignorant of the Kool-Aid swishers to see the scam that was Barack Obama.*

6.1 Vaporware

In the fledgling days of the personal computer industry, software vendors frequently announced products that were not yet ready for release. Some didn't even exist. The term "vaporware" was coined to describe this practice. Many of these announcements never became products. Some that did should not have.

The recent health-care reform known as ObamaCare is the modern-day, political version of vaporware.

6.2 Spaghetti Code

The VaporCare bill never reached the point where it was ready for "release." In software terminology, the legislation was nothing but "spaghetti code," as was the software designed to implement it. The bill and the code were designed by dozens of different people, all of whom brought their own styles, wants and objectives. There was no unifying objective to the legislation other than "we must have a new health care system and now!"

No one, including the writers of the bill, the Congress or President Obama, had an overall understanding of the legislation. It is doubtful whether anyone ever read the entire bill. The bill was a "living thing," changing when criticisms arose, decision-makers met or vote-buying was necessary. Few of the *ad hoc* changes had anything to do with improving the quality of health care.

By the end inconsistencies, deals, bribes, falsified data and outright lies had shaped the legislation and the public's perception of it. Despite its problems and unpopularity, health care reform moved forward. Congressional Democrats sacrificed the best health care system in the world and American taxpayers at the same time. No one in the political class knew what was in the final bill or whether the Frankenstein monster would work. Few cared.

Democrats passed the bill without a single Republican supporting vote. Little did they or their Messiah know at the time that **this bill doomed the Presidency and perhaps the Democrat Party itself.**

6.3 The Public Reaction

Vaporware or "sausage-making" might be foreign to voters, but their own health care is not. The public quickly realized that they did not matter, at least in the eyes of the political class. Passage of a bill, any bill, was more important than the quality or quantity of their health care.

Monument-building was too important a task for normal folks to be allowed input. The political elites knew what was best for the common folks, regardless of what the masses believed. They were intent on providing it, "good and hard."

Blinded by ambition, Democrats thought they could ignore the electorate. Despite rising public discontent, Democrats forged ahead. Their Holy Grail was within reach.

Democrats had a filibuster-proof majority. They designed (and continued to modify) ObamaCare with no input from Republicans or the public at large. Why not? Their President had messianic powers that would enable him to sell any program. It was a sure thing. Full speed ahead!

Democrats clearly misjudged. The largest ratings agency in the country, the voting public, rated the product defective. Despite objections, Democrats passed the bill.

Congress came across as imperial. President Obama fared no better.

6.4 Familiarity Breeds Contempt

President Obama's ego and self-absorption seemed to require him to be on stage all the time. According to CBS News[1], there were only 21 days in his first year where Obama did not make at least one public appearance. The statistics from CBS were amazing: 411 speeches, comments and remarks of which 52 were on VaporCare, 158 interviews, visits to 58 US cities and 21 foreign nations, 160 flights on Air Force One, 193 flights on Marine One, etc. etc. In short, **it was Obama time, all the time**.

While familiarity doesn't always breed contempt, incompetence does. President Obama was increasingly viewed as a disappointment. The economy did not respond as forecasted. Campaign promises were obviously untrue. Promised transparency became a joke. Foreign policy was seen wanting, embarrassing and dangerous. Terror defenses seemed weaker, Chicago-type deals were worked. Other real-world inconveniences intruded on "The One's" plan for his

---

[1]http://www.cbsnews.com/websites/2010/01/20/politics/politicalhotsheet/entry6119525.shtml

version of Camelot. These disappointments diminished the Obama mystique and wounded his Presidency.

6.5 The Slide Downhill

Obama's continued hard sell of the bill contained obvious lies. His performance revealed him to be little more than an unethical salesman attempting to foist off a defective product on what he considered to be a stupid group of customers. In Obama Wins Oscar[2], his style was compared to the motley sales force from the movie *Glengary Glen Ross*. There it was observed:

> Quite the performance, just not something most would expect from the President of the United States. The exchange seemed more appropriate for used car salesmen or "boiler-room" stock scams. In short, the performance seemed both desperate and dishonest. My thought was: "Would I buy aluminum siding from this man?"

ObamaCare cost Obama whatever credibility he had left. His campaign guise of nobility and omnipotence was revealed as fraudulent when he resorted to the tactics of an unethical used-car salesman. Messiahs don't sell snake oil. Anointed Ones don't engage in fraud.

The high hopes and dreams that accompanied Obama's ascendancy to the Presidency (and ultimately Mount Rushmore) came crashing down when he exposed his true self selling the ObamaCare lie. **His image changed from The Exalted Leader to just another Used Car Salesman from Chicago.**

Obama jokingly referred to the ending of the movie Thelma and Louise, saying health care would not end that way. But VaporCare

---

[2]http://www.economicnoise.com/2009/12/18/obama-wins-oscar/

did go over the cliff. **With it went what little remained of Obama's reputation, image and perhaps his Presidency.**

6.6 The Turning Point

ObamaCare tarnished all of its proponents. The Democrats experienced voter wrath in several special elections, none of which were expected to be, or should have been, close. The inexplicable losses seemed tied to the dissatisfaction with ObamaCare.

In a perverse and unintended way, ObamaCare united the country. The Left is angry and the Right is angry. Voting results suggested that Independents were leaving Democrats.

Polls portend further bad results ahead. That spells major problems for President Obama. **A political animal's first instinct is survival.** When re-election is jeopardized, watch out! Already one can see the Democrats distancing themselves from their President.

This President was likely doomed to failure without the ObamaCare debacle. However without it the realization of his shortcomings would not have come so soon. All style and no substance can fool some of the people some of the time. **Form and flair work in a campaign, but they are no substitute for governance.**

ObmaCare was an important tipping point. Visions of Obama's greatness were replaced with a tawdry picture of political opportunism and corruptness, self aggrandizement and Chicago-style gutter politics.

Stripped of his veneer, **Obama was seen to have no substance.** Some feared this outcome from the beginning, but hoped that charisma, myth and sizzle would suffice. It did not!

Obama quickly changed **from public celebrity to public nuisance.** Talented people may be tolerated for self-absorption and arrogance. Incompetents are not.

Obama's Presidency has been reduced from the Messianic to the tawdry, all as a result of ObamaCare. When his image died, so did his Presidency. Stick a fork in the Obama Presidency. It's ending began with ObamaCare.

The political excitement, however, is just beginning. The 2010 elections will not be pretty. Dems will be fighting for their political lives and running away from Obama. This will be cruel, much like a Mexican bullfight. Obama is the bull and the matadors come from his own party.

Like the bull, Obama will not comprehend what is happening. His self-image and former cult-like status will not allow it. His propensity toward anger and intolerance towards anyone in his way will make for a glorious, bloody fight. But **the matadors have both numbers and experience. They will finally overwhelm and kill the bull, but not without substantial losses in their own ranks.**

Bullfights are never pretty. Especially ones that drag on for years.

7 The President is Delusional

MARCH 15, 2010

President-of-the-World Obama is at it again. Apparently he feels the problems in this country are too small for him, or they have been solved. His wisdom and greatness are too important to be squandered on only one nation. They must be shared with the entire world.

In his latest initiative, Obama takes "I'm from the Government, and I'm here to help you" across national borders. Breitbart reports on the call for a conference on entrepreneurship:

> The White House on Friday announced a "summit on entrepreneurship" to build economic ties with the Islamic world, part of President Barack Obama's outreach to Muslims.

> The White House said it has invited participants from more than 40 countries over five continents for the April 26-27 conference in Washington.

On one level, this initiative is laughable, excellent fodder for Saturday Night Live and Jon Stewart skits. On another, it reflects a serious situation pertaining to **the continuing delusional nature of Obama and his Administration.**

7.1 Pathetic

The "summit" provides more face-time for the President, a Pavlovian response by this White House to all problems. Unfortunately, the public has soured on what is seen as Obama's endless campaigning. They want constructive action rather than platitudes and endless campaigning. "Talk is cheap" is an admonition this White House does not seem to understand.

Obama's approval numbers are in a downturn. At this stage, he is ahead in **the race to displace President Jimmy Carter as the worst president of the past several generations**. He provides Carter's ineptitude, without Carter's sincerity. Desperation regarding the unpopular health care bill is making Obama look like the next Joe Isuzu, the fictitious liar in Isuzu commercials. Truth must not stand in the way of a sale.

Does the White House not understand how farcical their actions have become? Are they clueless or incompetent? Both hypotheses fit the facts. Making a definitive choice between them is impossible and irrelevant.

President Obama now expects us to believe that he is Peter Drucker, the world's greatest management guru. This president has zero business experience and has surrounded himself with advisers similarly deficient in this area. Yet, they believe that they are **qualified to lecture the world on entrepreneurship**.

Would it be impolite to ask what he has done to further entrepreneurship in this country? What prescriptions or proposals has he provided to help entrepreneurs? Isn't small business in this country collapsing as a result of his policies?

If foreign leaders care at all about their economies, they will **run away** from this conference. **Investment and hiring in this country stopped when Obama's "solutions" rolled out.**

7.2 Delusional

We have a President who believes he is always the smartest man in the room, no matter what room. Actually, he is almost always the least experienced and least qualified in most rooms. The fact is that **he has no experience in anything.**

What is known of his background includes stints as a "community organizer" and adjunct professor. What skills are required to be a community organizer? What experience is needed? What experience is gained from such a position? Not surprisingly, none! At least none that is useful or transferable to a real job or executive role.

Obama's short stint as a lecturer on Constitutional Law was unremarkable in every academic sense. There is no evidence of writing or publishing. The most notable aspect was his interpretation of the Constitution as a "living document," open to changes that produce "social justice." In effect, other than as a quaint artifact of history, for Obama **the Constitution does not exist.**

Despite this vacuous background, **Obama believes he knows more about medicine than doctors, more about business than businessmen and more about creating jobs than entrepreneurs.** This sad litany could be continued but the point should be obvious. Obama believes **he has more to contribute than anyone else, on any topic, in any field.**

Any rational man with such limited background would defer to those wiser and more experienced. Instead, Obama presents himself to be an expert on all things. He is the modern-day political equivalent of Professor Irwin Corey, a comedian who billed himself as "The World's Foremost Authority" on everything. (For more on this man who made a career by synthesizing erudition and gibberish, google his name.)

Does Obama not see how ridiculous this behavior makes him look? What must audiences of accomplished doctors, businessmen or entrepreneurs think when this man-child with zero experience lectures them? One can imagine the disgust and anger they feel, and must repress.

"Don't worry, I stayed in a Holiday Inn Express last night" may work for TV but not as a governing strategy. Yet, Obama must believe that he received more than a good night's rest. He believes he is special, something larger than his office. A messianic image was part of his campaign. He still seems to believe it.

"The One" is an image clearly in conflict with reality. Acting the part is **delusional**.

I am not a psychologist or psychiatrist and do not pretend to have these skills. But any observant person will see the President's behavior as bizarre, if not outright dangerous. James Lewis[1] detailed the President's extreme narcissism and commented on the risk:

> The question is what real damage Obama may do to the country. This man has been entrusted with the greatest power in the world.

7.3 What If Obama Were Your Friend?

Obama's situation may be better understood on a human, as opposed to clinical, level. What would you do if your best friend believed that he was more knowledgeable than astrophysicists, oncologists, economists, businessmen, or other highly and specially-trained people?

What if he believed this so strongly that he felt he was entitled to "teach" or "lecture" practitioners in these highly specialized fields? As a friend, you would likely intervene and try to get him professional help. **Our President is this hypothetical friend.**

---

[1]http://www.americanthinker.com/2010/03/obamas_malignant_narcissism.html

Other Presidents have rebuked industries or professions. Eisenhower came down hard on the military-industrial complex; Kennedy did so with the steel industry. Others have chosen whipping boys for both good reasons and political ones. None, however, presumed they were smarter than everyone else. **Other than Obama, no one believed they had unique knowledge that was applicable anywhere and could improve everything.**

The President's behavior is delusional. While he sees himself as some modern-day, handsome version of Yoda, the rest of the nation is beginning to see him as "one sick puppy" who happens to hold the highest office in the land. He marches to a tune that others cannot hear.

Where are his friends, and why do they not intervene? Are they afraid to confront him with reality?

For the sake of the nation, if not for the sake of the man, someone should confront him about his problem. Delusional behavior is dangerous, especially when it affects the head of the world's most powerful country.

Does Obama not have a friend who will intervene? Is everyone around him a political toadie or ideologue willing to risk the safety of the country in order to advance their own personal or political goals?

8 Obama: Not Moses, Merely Elmer Gantry

SEPTEMBER 29, 2010

The abject failure of the Obama Administration is obvious. Herman Cain[1] described the situation:

> Millions of voters have come to realize that this presidency lacks leadership, direction, decisiveness, economic urgency and, most of all, solutions. This combination of deficiencies has produced a more than uninspired citizenry, except for the most loyal and misled supporters of the president.

While many recognize the failure, few appreciate the danger.

8.1 The Failure

The White House billed this summer as "the summer of recovery." **[It is now summer of 2014 and we are still waiting for a summer or any other season of recovery.]** To those who believed, this promise turned out to be a cruel joke. The phrase rapidly took its place among other memorable political phrases like "Read my lips," "Whip Inflation Now" and "Economic Malaise."

Despite obvious evidence to the contrary, the President blithely travels the land proclaiming economic success. Mr. Obama is either oblivious to reality or believes he is unaccountable for what he says.

---

[1]http://www.wnd.com/index.php?fa=PAGE.view&pageId=208429

The "white lies" of politics provide wide boundaries, yet Obama feels it is his right to widen them whenever it is convenient. Truth aside, how is it good politics to be telling folks who are hurting that things are just rosy?

Mr. Obama's narcissism and and messianic beliefs drive his behavior. Unfortunately, whatever magic he had is gone. Mr. Obama is now perceived as the emperor sans clothes. The public no longer sees Moses, but Elmer Gantry. Obama still believes he is Moses. This pathology is dangerous.

The recent CNBC town hall provided evidence of Obama's fall. Attendees were carefully screened. Most voted for Mr. Obama. The President played his role, but the cherry-picked audience did not buy it. The dissatisfaction and disillusionment was palpable. The defining moment was provided by Ms. Velma Hart:

> I'm a mother. I'm a wife. I'm an American veteran, and I'm one of your middle-class Americans. And quite frankly I'm exhausted. I'm exhausted of defending you, defending your administration, defending the mantle of change that I voted for, and deeply disappointed with where we are.

Softball-tossing John Harwell was unable to provide enough fat pitches for Mr. Obama to overcome the chagrin-drenched room. Only one person appeared to not understand what was happening. That person was the President. Even TOTUS, his teleprompter, had to know.

This is no recovery summer for the economy. Nor is there respite for the American people from the incessant preaching and onerous legislation coming from Washington. The White House economic team likely knows what is happening and are bailing out in advance.

Non-economic officials will also leave. The signs of the coming political and economic debacle are too obvious to miss. The population of rats on ships destined to sink always decreases in advance of the sinking. Rats instinctively know when it is time to leave. They are survivors.

Even "Baghdad Bob," a nickname for Robert Gibbs, previous Press Secretary, seems read to leave. His Iraqi counterpart shamelessly spun or dissembled up until the time US soldiers entered his TV studio. In similar fashion, Mr. Gibbs' loyalty did not crack until recently. As expressed in an article by Kurt Brouwer[2]:

> White House Press Secretary Robert Gibbs made a rather startling statement in a press briefing on September 21st. He acknowledged that the economy is bad and he further stated under questioning that the recovery would take several years.

These observations are important:

1. Our crackerjack media has mostly ignored the inconvenience of Mr. Gibbs' admission. Their complicity with this incompetent Administration is deplorable.
2. The economic mess could take decades to resolve.
3. Through the entire charade the President appears unaffected. He continues to pompously spout obvious untruths and exaggerations. Believing (correctly so far) that he owns the press, he has no fear of being called out. (What little respect he must have for the citizenry, expecting them to believe blatant lies!)

Enter reality. Supporters are disappointed and rebellious. Democrats are scared. They don't campaign on Obama's so-called accomplishments. Many of their political ads noticeably omit party affiliation.

---

[2]http://websites.marketwatch.com/fundmastery/2010/09/23/white-house-recovery-to-take-several-years/

The country is energized for the coming election which is likely to be epic. After the election is when danger for the President could begin to develop.

> **Addendum: It should be noted that Robert Gibbs' position was assumed by Jay Carney. In retrospect and in comparison, perhaps Mr. Gibbs should have been nicknamed Albert Einstein.**

8.2 Danger for Obama

The President is toxic. His poll numbers are dismal. Democrats are running from him. In a recent piece[3] it was joked that if a Democrat running for election had to appear in public with either Michael Vick or President Obama, he would choose Mr. Vick. [Michael Vick, a star quarterback, destroyed his reputation and marketability when he was convicted for raising dogs to fight in pits.] That is probable since Mr. Vick's considerable football skills appear to have returned.

This election will be the political equivalent of shock and awe. Media and Democrats will be confused and disorganized. Reports concerning the survivability of the party will follow. Republicans will not and should not be spared. Many of them deserve to be replaced. The unprincipled media, sensing the mood of the country, may no longer shill for the Democrat Party. Credibility, or what they have left of it, is the tool of their trade.

Serious danger may arise inside the Democrat Party. President Obama will be at the center of the storm. He is a newcomer, still viewed as an outsider. Obama was never personally popular among his peers; he was tolerated. To the extent that he advanced the agendas of those in power, he had value. Now his oratory and popularity no longer sell. He will be deemed responsible for the coming debacle.

---

[3]http://www.economicnoise.com/2010/09/22/michael-vick-or-barack-obama/

Obama is a liability. His aggressive agenda jeopardized the establishment. Presidents come and go but the old bulls of Congress die in office. It is they who own and run Washington, not some figurehead president. Obama's magic is gone. It duped the Party just as it did the country.

This wunderkind is now viewed as a pompous, dangerous fool by both sides of the aisle. He embarrasses the real power in Washington and is a potential threat to their political version of Cosa Nostra.

Political power is respected, even when it is disliked. Obama came into office displaying contempt for Congress. He established his own advisory group of czars. Congress was to be tolerated, but little more. Much of what was done was in violation of the Constitution. In a Congress where principles don't matter, advancing the ball is all that mattered.

Political alienation is never pretty. In this case, it could be tragic. We have a President with a Messiah complex, blinded by extreme narcissism. He has lived in an unreal bubble all his life, supported by shadowy figures who viewed him as a meal ticket for ideological change. Most of his life has been outside the realm of discipline and reality.

8.3 Danger for the Country

Mr. Obama has never experienced real failure or unpopularity. How will this abnormal, pampered man-child react to what may be total rejection? That is the problem. The President is likely a sociopath. The nation and his personal tragedy are inextricably linked. So is the Democrat Party. How this drama plays out could have serious ramifications for the entire world.

Mr. Obama is unlikely to handle adversity well. His two-year record contains too many examples of pettiness and "it's-never-my-fault" behavior. Whether he behaves as a spoiled brat and strikes out at some country (say Iran) to demonstrate his manhood is unknowable. Perhaps he will surprise and accept the fact that he has replaced Jimmy Carter as our worst President, although that seems highly unlikely.

An intervention seems inevitable. It might be from trusted friends or it could be a Nixonian pre-resignation meeting. The Democrat Party will intervene out of self-interest rather than concern for the tragedy we call Mr. President. This meeting is likely to be of the Nixonian type.

Obama's initial reaction is predictable. The President and his Chicago thugs will resist. These are tough guys, but from a small pond. The amateurs from Chicago don't stand much of a chance against the Washington pros.

This matchup is one-sided. It is street-crime versus organized crime.

II THE UNLIKELY RE-ELECTION

The Democrats got clobbered in the 2010 mid-terms. It was a wave election. They lost the House but retained the Senate (some say as a result of Republican ineptness).

State-level elections were even more historic. State control moved toward Republicans in waves. Republicans gained control in some states for the first time in a century.

Democrats were soundly rejected at every level. The future for Barack Obama did not appear bright. His continuing problems are covered in this section, as is his surprising (and still perplexing) re-election.

9 Why the Democrat Party Cannot Survive

NOVEMBER 17, 2010

After the election two years ago, Time Magazine questioned whether the Elephant had become an extinct political animal. The most recent election raised questions as to whether the Donkey should be deemed an endangered species. Questioning either party's extinction helps sell news. However one or two elections are not sufficient for claiming trends and certainly insufficient for making survival judgments.

Political parties are not immortal. They are born and eventually die. Survivability is dependent upon Darwinian-type adaptations rather than a genetically-determined life span. Length of existence is determined by strategy and tactics rather than cellular aging.

Immediate change in the American landscape is coming. The "pendulum theory" of politics – one party disappoints, is removed and then returned when the other party disappoints – is simplistic, but often predictive of short-term trends. Peggy Noonan[1] recently used this approach to explain what she viewed as short-term change within a stable long-term framework.

Viewing matters on a longer-term basis requires a different approach. Strategy rather than tactics dominate survival considerations.

Strategy evaluation suggests the Democrat Party is vulnerable and could be headed for extinction. These considerations have little to do with the 2010 election results. Nor do the 2010 election results have much bearing on longer-term survival considerations.

---

[1]http://online.wsj.com/article/SB10001424052748703848204575608453836688106.html

9.1 The Meaning of the Recent Elections

In the two most recent elections, each political party was soundly rejected but for different reasons. Simply and bluntly:

- **The Republicans were tossed out because they did not govern according to their principles.**
- **The Democrats were tossed out because they did govern according to their principles.**

One party lost because it **misbehaved**; the other because it **revealed itself**.

Obama's election was erroneously interpreted as a mandate for radical change by left-wing loonies. In spite of his uniqueness, Obama's election was more a vote against Republican spending, hypocrisy and general misbehavior.

Socialist Obama unwisely interpreted his election as a mandate to impose his ideology on the country. His overreach scared many and unleashed fears of the coercive behavior about which George Washington famously warned:

> Government is not reason; it is not eloquent; it is force.
> Like fire, it is a dangerous servant and a fearful master.

Government arrogance and arbitrariness initiated a groundswell of concern that coalesced into the Tea Party movement. Ridiculed by the elites in both major parties, the Tea Party provided an outlet for voter rage, a point still not properly understood by the establishment.

The Tea Party is a threat to both established parties not because it represents a third-party movement. It is less a political movement than a means of expressing frustration against both parties. Its threat lies in the fact that it reflects a popular movement to re-establish the Constitution. Neither party wants that.

The 2010 election was a referendum on Obama and his extremist policies. The Democrat raw grasp for power likely ensures they will not do well in the next few elections. This judgment reflects the simplistic pendulum view of politics.

Strategic considerations suggest that both parties should fear the future, but especially Democrats.

9.2 Party Principles

The alleged principles of both major parties need to be understood. "Alleged" is a necessary modifier because these principles are little more than marketing props to be displayed when useful and otherwise ignored. Groucho Marx captured the essence of both political parties when he discussed principles:

> Those are my principles, and if you don't like them, well I have others.

Republican principles are closer to George Washington's view of government – government is necessary but dangerous. Hence, it is best kept small and weak. Republicans claim to stand for limited government because it allows for maximum individual freedom. These principles require a governing model that focuses on less tax, less spending and less regulation. The key word is "less" as in less government.

Democrat principles are based on the assumption that government is a force for good. Government is presumed necessary to help individuals and ensure "social justice," (a term impossible to reasonably define). This philosophy leads to bigger government as in more spending, more taxes and more regulatory control. For Democrats, the key word is "more" as in more government.

Republicans have deviated more from their stated principles than Democrats. In an effort to win more elections, they became Democrat-lite.

9.3 Winning Versus Governing

Getting elected (and then re-elected) is the primary political motivation of both parties. But **getting elected and governing are two different activities**. Party principles should serve both. Often they serve one better than the other. Content from a reader email cleverly illustrated the point:

> Two third-graders are running for class president. Johnny's platform includes a detailed program to improve various school matters and a commitment to work hard. His opponent, Mary, promises free ice cream for everyone. Mary is elected by an overwhelming margin.

Johnny's election strategy is similar to that of Republicans. Mary's is similar to that of Democrats. Sacrifice, abstinence and/or self-reliance are political "root canals" when compared to "freebies."

The success of the Democrat "ice cream" strategy is best understood via some simple statistics. In the 66 years from 1945 forward, Democrats controlled both Houses of Congress and the presidency for twenty years, and Republicans six years. Democrats controlled both Houses for 44 years, and Republicans fourteen years, with ten of those since 1995.

The "ice cream" strategy was implemented by Franklin D. Roosevelt in the US in the 1930s. (It was originally invented by Otto von Bismarck in the 1880s.)

Arguably, this strategy created the modern Democrat Party. It rescued a floundering party and enabled it to dominate. **From a** political standpoint, the strategy was pure genius. From an economic standpoint, it produced slower growth than otherwise would have occurred.

In an effort to compete in elections Republicans adopted a "yogurt" or "ice-cream lite" strategy. That is, they were dragged down into the same giveaway strategy that was so successful for Democrats. They didn't play it as well or offer as much.

9.4 Governance Problems

One problem with the "ice cream" strategy is that one cannot provide ice cream to everyone. There isn't enough ice cream to go around. Even if there were, one would need to discriminate in terms of portions, because the strategy is dependent on unequal treatment as the means to create interest or constituency groups.

Democrats utilize the strategy in exchange for votes. Groups likely to respond to ice cream are targeted and promises made. The end result is a motley collection of beneficiaries "bought" at various times and in various ways. These include minorities, government employees, big labor, trial lawyers, teacher unions, gays, radical women's groups and environmentalists among others.

The lack of commonality among these groups presents a problem. What is provided to one means less is available for another. Tension between groups must always be managed. This tension surfaced recently when Democrats began to focus on Hispanics. Blacks considered this attention a threat to their importance and claims.

Governing presents a more difficult problem. Interest group politics is not conducive to effective and fair governing. It demands favorable treatment for some and not others. That in itself guarantees bad governance. Political leaders are supposed to represent all the people in their district, state or country.

Equal treatment is impossible with an election strategy based on discrimination. Governance must be focused on a portion of the population rather than the entire population. Even within that portion, inequality must exist in order to properly manage the sub-groups.

The strategy requires governing not "for the people," but "for some of the people," and even then not equally within the sub-group. Such governance is not fair and inconsistent with the concept of equal treatment under the law. Yet the Democrats have utilized it successfully for eighty years.

Democrats claim the Republicans have done the same as the "party of the rich." Whether that is a defensive claim by Democrats to divert attention from their approach to governing is left to the reader to decide. The important point is that the Democrats developed the strategy, used it effectively and benefited enormously from it.

9.5 The Fatal Flaw

There is a fatal flaw in the ice cream strategy. The strategy depends on a continuing and increasing availability of goodies. **Once you run out of ice cream, you can no longer buy or maintain your "clients."** Lady Thatcher expressed it this way:

> The trouble with Socialism is, sooner or later you run out of other people's money.

Thatcher's end point has arrived in the US and other Social Welfare States). For eighty years government grew disproportionately faster than the economy. The Democrat "ice cream" strategy was responsible for much of this growth.

The continuance of such growth is mathematically limited. There are limited resources to hand out. At some point, the increasing "takers" want more than the decreasing "makers" are able or willing to provide.

That point has been reached or is very near in the US and other Social Welfare States. That is the reason why new programs are not funded by tax increases. The productive sector cannot tolerate additional burdens. Instead, governments desperate to continue their charade resort to debt and the printing of money. But this chicanery cannot continue much longer.

9.6 The Ice Cream is Gone

Welfare states around the world are all facing the problem of insolvency. Welfare State R.I.P.[2] discussed the debt burdens and this problem in detail. It is mathematically impossible to honor all the promises. **The ice cream is gone and with it the key to 80 years of Democrat success.**

Many voters understand the government is insolvent. That knowledge was the driving force behind the Tea Party. While no one wants their goodies reduced or removed, growing numbers recognize that government growth must slow, stop or even reverse.

This reality is potentially devastating for Democrats. Holding a disparate coalition together was difficult enough when ice cream was plentiful. **Holding them together when funds are being cut may be impossible.**

The Democrats have no coherent message other than bigger government and more benefits. Both parts of that message will soon be invalidated by circumstances and lack of resources.

The Democrat coalition is likely too fragmented to hold under a **governing** rather than an **electing** strategy. The groups are so conditioned to "more" that it is unlikely that they can be maintained under the "less" strategy that is soon to be forced on them.

It is not impossible for the Democrat Party to survive. It will not be easy, however. If there is a strategy that they might successfully

---

[2]http://www.economicnoise.com/?p=9491

adopt, it is that **we will give you less than you got before but more than the other guys**. With so many voters sucking on the government teat, it is difficult to judge how effective that approach might be. There are no other political options that appear to be viable.

A major overhaul of both political parties is coming. I suspect the Democrats will not survive. **My guess is that the Republicans will become the party of the left, although not much left of where they are today**. A new party on the right will emerge, probably based on an original interpretation of the Constitution. Many Democrats will migrate to the Republican Party while some Republicans will migrate to the new party. Life will go on.

The realignment will be slow and evolve over decades. It will formalize the major shift rightward that has been occurring in the country for years. The people moving in this direction have been frustrated by lack of an outlet for their vote. The emergence of a new political party will provide this outlet.

With the ice cream gone or limited, politicians will have to cater to voters rather than bribe them. Similar trends are occurring in Europe where the Welfare State is spent. A long, slow rollback is necessary and about to begin.

The alternative, continuing on the current path, leads to economic and societal collapse.

10 President Quixote's Legacy

JUNE 28, 2011

The enthusiasm for Obama appears inversely related to his time in office. Many wonder what happened to "The One We Are Waiting For."

Obama assumed office in difficult economic times. After a couple of years of excuses, which included "the problems were worse than we knew" and the generic, all-purpose "it's Bush's fault," Obama now owns the problems, including new ones of his own making.

An incomplete report of Obama's "accomplishments" includes the following:

- the economy worsened
- discretionary military efforts ("kinetic" is the word the Administration used) increased
- an unpopular, flawed health care plan was forced on the public
- inflation increased, especially in critical goods like food and gasoline
- job prospects decreased
- the stimulus failed miserably
- "transparency in government" became a laugh-line for late night TV
- Chicago-style politics added to government corruption
- the housing problem worsened with no signs of ending
- government debt and spending spun out of control

- Wall Street was bailed out and enriched
- Main Street was ignored and became poorer
-
- race relations worsened

This list is not complete, but damning enough. Other than the demise of Osama bin Laden, it is difficult to point to anything positive.

10.1 What Happened?

Two hypotheses are cited to explain the sad state of affairs:

1. Obama is incompetent.
2. Obama knows what he is doing and is deliberately destroying the country.

These hypotheses are not mutually exclusive. Evidence can be found supporting both.

The remainder of this article deals only with the incompetence issue. Readers should not assume that the second is unimportant or inoperable.

10.2 Thomas Sowell's Insight

Dr. Thomas Sowell's insights about "seductive beliefs[1]" is especially valuable. He described some of the incorrect beliefs guiding President Obama. The bottom line is that Obama is an ideologue, narrowly and poorly educated. As a result, he is ignorant in the truest sense of the word.

---

[1]http://townhall.com/columnists/thomassowell/2011/05/31/seductive_beliefs/page/full/

It is important to differentiate between "ignorant" and "stupid." Ignorance results from lack of exposure. Obama's educational opportunities provided him with exposure relatively few others have. He had the opportunity to overcome ignorance, but apparently not the inclination. He either chose to ignore this opportunity or was unable to comprehend what was available. Either alternative sounds more like "stupidity" than "ignorance."

10.3 Economics versus Morality

Sowell's analysis provides insight on Obama's behavior. Obama has virtually no understanding of basic economics. Exploitation ideology is the basis for his world and economic view. This ideology sees the world as a zero-sum game. In essence a fixed pie is available. If one person gets more, others necessarily get less.

The wealth of nations is explained similarly. A country becomes successful by taking advantage of other countries. This naive view, based on the long discredited concept of mercantilism, sees **success as exploitation**. Freedom, markets, institutions, incentives, effort or any other important economic determinants are missing and unimportant in Obama's view of the world. Success or failure is determined by a single condition – whether you are the exploiter or the exploited.

Exploitation theory does not comport with economic theory, history or reality. As Sowell points out:

> It is hard to reconcile "exploitation" theories with the facts. While there have been conquered peoples made poorer by their conquerors, especially by Spanish conquerors in the Western Hemisphere, in general most poor countries were poor for reasons that existed before the conquerors arrived. Some Third World countries are poorer today than they were when they were ruled by Western countries, generations ago.

Obama's ideology blinds him to the relevant variables. Incentives, institutional frameworks, profit and loss, individual initiative, savings, investment, hard work, etc. play no role in his simplistic view of the way things work. That is why his economic policies have been such failures. He is unable to see that people respond to signals, incentives and disincentives.

Obama is a political and ideological creature. He does not understand markets, business, meeting a payroll or managing an organization. His knowledge/skills vacuum produces economic failure because his policies ignore the truly relevant variables. His ideology blinds him from seeing anything outside a Marxist lens.

Obama's view of success is especially perverse. **Success and failure are viewed as moral rather than economic outcomes.** Success is a marker for evil. It results from someone exploiting another. Failure is due to someone else's success rather than personal shortcomings. Economic success is the equivalent of immoral behavior. Proper moral behavior results in economic disadvantage.

In his simplistic world, economics is inconsistent with morality. Hence economics itself must be immoral and evil. This view is beyond simple and ignorant. It represents stupidity of the first order!

Recognition of these stupidity is key to understanding Obama's behavior and policies.

10.4 Beliefs and Actions

Moral judgments drive Obama's domestic policy. Individual success for some results in the economic failure of others. That explains Obama's "Joe the Plumber" moment. If the pie is fixed in size, the rich make others poor. That is the fallacy buttressing Obama's belief that people are entitled to only so much income or wealth. That is the basis for his moral imperative to redistribute income and wealth. They are ill-gotten gains.

This confused mindset also explains his foreign policy. Successful allies (think Israel and Great Britain among others) are morally inferior to unsuccessful, backward nations. The latter are poor because the richer nations exploited them. Third-world nations deserve restitution for the evils imposed by successful nations. That some of these are enemies of the US only makes them more deserving.

The US, the greatest economic success, represents the greatest evil and exploiter. Obama's world-apology tours and (mis)treatment of allies can be understood in light of this nonsense.

In his mind, Obama has the moral obligation to confiscate and redistribute wealth. This delusional modern-day version of Don Quixote believes his mission is to punish the rich and successful for their immoral behavior.

Talent, hard work, ingenuity, risk-taking etc., are foreign and irrelevant to Obama's third-grade-level of understanding human behavior. Thomas Sowell explains it:

> Whether at home or abroad, Obama's ideology is an ideology of envy, resentment and payback.

10.5 The Bigger Problem

Obama is doing what he believes right and just. Sophomoric understanding, however, does not explain why the inequities of the world are assumed to be Obama's responsibility. How does one go from President of the US to a modern day Don Quixote for the entire world?

Some psychologists and psychiatrists answer this question in terms of Obama's ego and pathological narcissism. The psychological conditions that motivate a person are less clear than the actions they take. Actions are visible, motivation is not. To understand a person and to anticipate how he will act, it is necessary to speculate on the psychological conditions that motivate him.

Obama's narcissistic disorder enables him to see himself as the President of The World, the Great Rectifier and the One We Are Waiting For. Some supporters speak of Obama in messianic terms, as he himself has arrogantly done. This behavior is suggestive of severe delusion, even megalomania.

The original Don Quixote's tilting at windmills was charming and harmless. The knight of old was noble and honorable. He possessed character and integrity. Even though a bit crazed, his motives were pure. It was difficult not to admire him in spite of his bizarre behavior.

None of that is true for President Quixote. The only thing these two delusional people have in common is a fascination with windmills. The old knight imagined them as dragons to be slain; the modern one as solutions to the world's environmental problems.

Obama's faults are neither charming nor harmless. He is in possession of extreme power and capable of doing massive damage. His misguided behavior squanders the nation's resources and commits future generations to lower standards of living. Obama, like his predecessor of old, intends to solve all the injustices of the world. His Quest is to correct the sins of the successful.

The downtrodden are Obama's protectorate, or so he claims. This modern Quixote, however, exploits them for political gain. Make them dependent and helpless so that they will vote for more government. This is not noble behavior. This deliberate destruction of lives is for personal advantage and power.

10.6 Obama's Superior Intellect

How dangerous this delusional man might be is moot. What seems no longer at issue is Obama's "superior intelligence." Obama's belief system is dominated by the dismissed exploitation theories of Karl Marx and the 60's style radicals he grew up around.

The Reverend Wright, preached to him for twenty years about exploitation in terms of Black Liberation Theology. An unrepentant terrorist, Bill Ayers was a close friend and arguably author of one of Obama's autobiographies. His personally selected "Czars" are the sorriest collection of Presidential advisors ever, at least in terms of reflecting American values and beliefs.

Many went on the same intellectual voyage that Obama did. Most outgrew it, usually by their mid-twenties. Obama never did. He is still a child, intellectually undeveloped and locked into the ideas from the 60's – both the 1960s and the Marxist 1860s. In that sense **he is an intellectual dwarf, frozen in a state of intellectual puberty**. His "knowledge" is based on nothing but the discredited ideologies of Socialism.

The claim that Obama is the smartest man to ever hold presidential office is absurd and a sad reflection on anyone holding this belief. Obama's obsession with keeping his college records and personal past secret seems to provide *prima facie* evidence that the claim is untrue. His knowledge base and dismal performance on the world stage is even more damning in this regard.

Instead of having a superior intellect, we likely have **the most ignorant, ideological, brainwashed dupe this country has ever elected to high office**. The man's intellectual development never progressed beyond the stage of all-night freshman bull sessions where all the world's problems were solved (with help from adequate amounts of beer or drugs).

This intellectual pygmy should be removed from office by whatever possible peaceful means. Impeachment is in order, but will not likely happen. Thus the 2012 election is critical.

The Democrat Party knows what happened in 2010. They also know that they have an albatross at the top of their ticket. It is likely they will turn on this poseur before the election. If so, this act will be their most significant public service in years.

Obama will not be re-elected, but that may not be enough. [Sadly, this prediction was off the mark.] A country filled with enough fools to elect this modern day version of a snake oil salesman, this American Idol wannabe, this empty suit, is clearly dumb enough to replace him in kind.

H. L. Mencken had it correct:

> Democracy is a form of worship. It is the worship of jackals by jackasses

The Democrat Party is and should be worried about 2012. No Democrat, save the hapless Jimmy Carter, can be happy about their current situation. Carter is the exception because his lock on "worst President ever" is about to be assumed by the current occupant of the White House.

11 Will Scandal Drive Obama Off the 2012 Ticket?

SEPTEMBER 21, 2011

President Obama may not run in 2012. That prediction seems reasonable in light of the following:

1. His presidency is in shambles, shriveling up before our eyes.
2. Political polls continue to weaken.
3. Unemployment remains stubbornly high for a period of time not seen since the Great Depression.
4. The economy is listless, consumer sentiment is in the sewer, foreclosures are ratcheting up and the next financial crisis could be near.
5. No major economic variable has improved; many continue to worsen.
6. The nation risks sovereign bankruptcy as a result of Obama's out of control spending.
7. Obama is out of ideas and obviously well beyond his depth.

Every time Obama speaks, he shows himself more out of touch with the country, its people and its ideals. He is an embarrassment to many, alienating independents and even some liberals.

Obama now appears to have adopted a strategy to appeal to the most radical in his party. Either he is trying to avoid a shut-out in the coming election by locking up some small number of votes or he is delusional. Seasoned Democrats are dumbfounded by his performance, seeming to believe the delusional possibility. Radicals threaten to run a competing candidate against him in the primaries.

Nothing fazes The Narcissist-In-Chief who needs the spotlight like most of us need oxygen. Obama intends to run in 2012. Messiahs, or at least this self-proclaimed "One," do not see problems. Problems to them are mere details and trivialities to be silver-tongued away.

Obama is spent. His magic is no more. He has become a cartoon caricature for many Americans and foreigners. Familiarity has produced contempt. He is a fraud, a man who never was anything other than a carefully scripted and wonderfully executed marketing campaign.

The product, however, doesn't work. Marketing made the first sale, but repeat purchases occur only if the product performs. **Snake oil is never purchased a second time**. Instead of the brilliant problem-solving uniter expected, the nation got an incompetent, small, and not likable mountebank.

Obama lives in his own world, surrounded by sycophants. They may know his run is over and that he no longer fools most of the people. Yet they are likely afraid to tell him. A modern day political tragedy, not unlike the one that consumed Richard Nixon, is developing.

Obama sees none of this. It has never entered his mind that he is a failure or will not run. His supporters, namely the Democrat Party and the mainstream media, may intervene. Their survival and credibility may demand it. There may come a "meeting with Nixon" moment. If that fails, and it is very likely to, Obama will be destroyed by one or both of these two groups.

11.1 Party Interests

The political environment is horrible for Democrats. Obama's policies, ineptness and unpopularity are responsible. Many elected

Democrats are afraid for their political careers. Obama is seen as a drag in the coming election.

Previously unthinkable election "upsets" have already occurred, The loss of the "Kennedy Seat" in Massachusetts was the first. The 2010 mid-terms represented a historic rout. Subsequent special elections affirmed that the trend continues. Jonah Goldberg[1] commented on the most recent:

> ... the seat that once belonged to Geraldine Ferraro, Chuck Schumer and Anthony Weiner went to Republican Bob Turner the first time it has gone Republican since 1923.

The idea of Obama resigning for the good of the party has been raised. Steve Chapman[2] of the Chicago Tribune said:

> Obama might do his party a big favor. In hard times, voters have a powerful urge to punish incumbents. He could slake this thirst by stepping aside and taking the blame. Then someone less reviled could replace him at the top of the ticket.

About a year ago, political cannibalism[3] was predicted:

> The next two years will be hard on Obama. As much as he is hated by freedom-lovers in the country, it is likely that he will be hated more by his remaining Democrats. The Party is in tatters. It is in danger of disappearing as a political entity as a result of following

---

[1]http://www.nypost.com/p/news/opinion/opedcolumnists/obama_in_winter_xGE1fA0MUHOUdfHaABQCAP

[2]http://www.realclearpolitics.com/articles/2011/09/19/why_obama_should_withdraw_111374.html

[3]http://www.economicnoise.com/?p=15371

this false prophet. This Pied Piper, instead of getting the American people to follow, led Democrat politicians to their political death. The survivors will not forget, nor will they continue to march to the tune of this false savior.

We are about to witness politics at its ugliest. It will be Republicans against Democrats of course. But that will be less intriguing than Democrats against Obama. Political survival trumps loyalty – every time! If Obama is as ineffectual as I believe, he is likely to be devoured by angry Democrats anxious to avenge the political deaths of their comrades and the damage done to the Party.

We have reached the point where **Democrats have the motive to get rid of Obama, but do they have the means or ability?**

11.2 Solyndra

Solyndra, the "green energy" failure, is one example of how Obama might be leveraged out of office. Chicago-style politics suggests there may be other scandals in this same closet or other closets.

Reuters[4] described Solyndra as follows:

> The bankruptcy of solar-panel maker Solyndra neatly encapsulates the economic, political and intellectual bankruptcy of Barack Obama's Big Idea. It was the president's intention back in 2009 to begin centrally reorganizing the U.S. economy around the supposed climate-change crisis.

> Even after getting the loan, Solyndra spent $187,000 on lobbying efforts, according to Bloomberg,[5] including

---

[4] http://websites.reuters.com/james-pethokoukis/2011/09/16/solyndra-the-logical-endpoint-of-obamanomics/

[5] http://www.bloomberg.com/news/2011-09-16/solyndra-lobbied-white-house-for-solar-panels-on-u-s-buildings.html

trying to get the White House to push government agencies to install its panels on the rooftops of federal buildings and extend "buy American" rules that favor U.S. companies. Instead of revenue seeking, Solyndra was "rent seeking," which means trying to make money by manipulating government .

Andrew C. McCarthy[6] described Solyndra as criminal fraud:

The Solyndra debacle is not just Obama-style crony socialism as usual. It is a criminal fraud. That is the theory that would be guiding any competent prosecutor's office in the investigation of a scheme that cost victims in this case, American taxpayers, a fortune.

The magnitude of the Solyndra loss needs investigation. The mood of the country demands it. Taxpayers are furious about Washington wasting their money and indebting their children. This single company represents one half billion wasted, under questionable circumstances. How many other similar "deals" might be heading for the same fate.

Political chicanery of this magnitude should not be ignored. The FBI jumped in early. According to Politico[7] other investigations are underway:

There are at least four investigations running on the legal, political and financial ties between the Obama administration and the California solar company that filed for bankruptcy protection last month.

It is likely that Solyndra contains enough incriminating information for Congress to force Obama from office (see Zerohedge[8], especially

---

[6]http://www.nationalreview.com/articles/277512/solyndra-fraud-andrew-c-mccarthy
[7]http://www.politico.com/news/stories/0911/63654.html#ixzz1Y7Ac4uVA
[8]http://www.zerohedge.com/news/why-was-congress-forced-subpoena-head-obamas-budget-office-get-info-solyndra

the slide show). There are other Solyndras out there in the "green energy" area. There are also other scandals beyond "green energy."

11.3 Congressional Investigations

Congressional investigations are typically held for Washington tourists. Rarely are these dog and pony shows serious. When a President is suspected of extreme stupidity or a crime, it is conventional for his party to do everything possible to thwart the investigation. Bill Clinton provided the most recent example.

Many Democrats would like to rid themselves of Albatross Obama. Under normal circumstances it might not be possible without risking the alienation of key constituencies. A criminal investigation, however, provides cover for modern-day regicide.

The Solyndra investigations (or whatever other scandals pop up) may be different. Congressional Democrats may view their own situation as worse if they protect the man rather than dump him. Under such circumstances Solyndra or a similar scandal could become a true bi-partisan search for the truth.

Democrats might even have incentives to be more aggressive than Republicans. None of these speculations are based on integrity, ethics, the pursuit of justice or the Rule of Law. The driver is political self-interest and survival.

Appearing tough in such an investigation serves to distance Democrats from their titular head. If there is a smoking gun, Democrats may pursue it. If they see an opportunity to take out the King, they may go for it. Their reaction will be one determined by their assessment of what is in their best interests, not the country or the Rule of Law.

11.4 The Media

Barack Obama won the Democrat nomination because the mainstream media adopted him and went out of their way to ensure that he, rather than Hillary Clinton, won. As expressed by the National Post[9]:

> American journalism will have to look back at the period starting with Barrack [sic] Obama's rise, his assumption of the presidency and his conduct in it to the present, and ask itself how it came to cast aside so many of its vital functions. In the main, the establishment American media abandoned its critical faculties during the Obama campaign and it hasn't reclaimed them since.

The press pushed an untried, unknown and incompetent man on the American republic. Media preferences are responsible for America's disaster.

Foreign policy is now a blend of confusion and costly impotence. America is increasingly bypassed or derided in the world. The great approach to the Muslim world, symbolized by the Cairo speech, is in tatters. Domestically, America's debt and deficits are an existential burden for itself and the global economy. And the occupant of the White House is becoming a laughingstock.

The press neglected its traditional function as referee and watchdog. It became a cup-bearer for its Styrofoam demigod. It pushed Obama ahead of Hillary Clinton, becoming an accomplice in the flaws and failures of what is one of the most miserable performances in the history of the American presidency.

A tipping point may have appeared in the last month or so. The myth of Obama has ended. There is now open talk that Obama cannot win in 2012.

---

[9] http://fullcomment.nationalpost.com/2011/09/17/rex-murphy-the-medias-love-affair-with-a-disastrous-president/

No Democrat sympathizer wants a pariah at the top of the ticket. Many in the media recognize the current problem and do not want to continue plugging what is obviously a failed president.

The protective shield appears to be weakening. Both the party and the media are becoming more concerned about saving what credibility they have left, rather than defending an increasingly indefensible and broken presidency.

Investigative reporting, obviously missing when Obama was The Next Coming, may become important again. The media will cover real Congressional investigations should they occur. Entrepreneurs within their ranks may focus on filling in the blanks in Obama's past. The rewards for becoming the next Woodward or Bernstein are immense. The chance to "change history" is an overpowering incentive for cub and seasoned reporters.

If it becomes acceptable to question this protected President, look for lots of new information to come out. There are a lot of closets with doors that have been sealed tight. If these are pried open, there may be some ugly discoveries.

11.5 Conclusion

This is a dangerous period for the President. His two biggest support groups have decreasing incentives to support him. If matters continue to deteriorate, they may have incentives to get rid of him. Should Congressional investigations become real, they likely will.

Real investigations do not mean President Obama will not get a fair shake. Justice, perhaps for the wrong reasons, would be getting a fair shake. That is usually harmful for any politician under investigation.

Loyalty in politics starts and stops with personal self-interest. The old saying, "If you want a friend in Washington, get a dog," still holds. Obama has few friends, even in his own party. Fortunately he has a dog. I hope it likes him, because much of the country no longer does.

How does it end? My guess is that investigations go forward and are used to leverage Obama out of office. He could "choose" not to run for re-election. He understands Chicago-style politics, even when he is on the wrong end of it.

His psyche is such that he must be loved, if not worshiped. That will never again be, at least not in this country.

12 A Failed Legacy

SEPTEMBER 15, 2011

President Obama is a political train wreck. Democrat careers are on the line as a result. Most will be distancing themselves from their former meal ticket.

Let the rationalizations begin, but they will be unable to hide this reality.

12.1 The Recent Election

The race to replace Anthony Weiner (truly irreplaceable) is over. Congressional district NY-9 was to have been a slam-dunk for Democrats. It was a district that had not elected a Republican in ninety years, one of the more liberal districts in the country.

The outcome showed that no Democrat is safe any more, anywhere. The results provided another dent in what was once-considered invincible Democrat armor. Scott Brown taking the "Ted Kennedy seat" in Massachusetts was the first example of this vulnerability.

Lame duck is a term usually reserved for politicians when they are ineligible to run again. Even though Obama is eligible to run for a second term, it seems applicable. Perhaps, the way things are shaping up, "dead duck" might be more appropriate.

The mainstream media is beside itself trying to rationalize the congressional race in NY-9. From Chriss W. Street[1] comes this report:

---

[1] http://www.breitbart.com/Big-Government/2011/09/14/New-York-Fallout--President-Obama-Moving-to-Avoid-Political-Suicide

The ultra-liberal Huffington Post blared that President Obama: "MOVING TO AVOID POLITICAL SUICIDE"; as the White House abandoned efforts to pass his American Jobs Act and went into a maximum defensive mode to save the President's imploding re-election campaign following the loss of Anthony Weiner's ultra-Democrat New York House seat and the launch of an inter-party rebellion to deny Obama the Democratic nomination for President.

Much of the blame can be attributed to the dismal performance of President Obama. But the media and Democratic enthusiasts, still in denial, offer other excuses — Democrats had a weak candidate, the economy was to blame, Obamacare still riles people, Weiner should have bowed out more gracefully, the treatment of Israel was responsible and on and on. An interesting rationale comes from Mickey Kaus[2] who suggests the result was due to a tactical error by Obama:

> It's the possibility that the Democrats favorite issue–Social Security–didn't work to save them because Obama, too, has embraced cutting Social Security and Medicare in "some undefined 'everything on the table' entitlement reform," as Weigel puts it. Could it be that the differences between Obama's Medicare cuts and GOP Rep. Paul Ryan's Medicare cuts–differences that seem so significant to policy analysts in Washington (and to me)–don't have much salience in the crude argumentation of direct-mail electioneering? Now that's scary for a Dem. After decades of pledging not to touch the two sacred programs, it's beginning to look as if Democrats can't just suddenly agree to pull trillions

---

[2]http://dailycaller.com/2011/09/14/what-really-terrifies-dems-about-ny-9/#ixzz1XwbyedcE

out of Social Security and and expect voters to maintain their reflexive loyalties.

This perspective is floated by others as well. If one accepts it, then matters are worse than they seem for Democrats. To believe that some poorly defined concession by Obama that the US has limited funds could cause such a political earthquake is to implicitly admit that Democrat popularity depends on supplying more "goodies" than Republicans.

No doubt the "goodies" hypothesis explains part (much?) of the Democrat appeal, but it is irrelevant in explaining these recent elections. It is hard to believe that a half-century of Democrat brainwashing with respect to Republicans wiping out their social security could be erased by a casual remark. Does any Democrat believe that their benefits are "safer" with Republicans than Democrats? Democrats have demagogued this issue for decades and their demagoguery has been reinforced by a complicit media.

If the Social Security hypothesis were correct, the results of the NY election imply there is no reason to vote Democrat if they cannot provide more benefits. Apparently the mere suggestion by Obama that Santa Claus died and "entitlements" must be looked at is enough to cause lifetime Democrat voters to stay home or to vote for the Grinch party.

More citizens realize that Santa Claus died and that cutbacks will be coming. Republicans may be seen as more serious about cutting spending than Democrats. If so, some may perceive them as creating enough savings elsewhere to better insulate Social Security promises. Such logic seems to far removed from the normal Democrat calculus.

Regardless of the underlying reasons, the results shocked Democrats.

12.2 Obama's Gift

To blame the outcome of this election on misplaying the Social Security card seems far-fetched. More plausible is a hypothesis that this election was a reaction to extreme Liberalism (Socialism).

Socialism has always been popular as a Utopian fantasy. Obama has begun to show that Socialism implemented does not mean the fantasies. Experience reveals dystopia.

The siren song of Socialism is its virtue. Up close and personal, it doesn't look or feel so good. It has failed and made life less enjoyable, if not downright miserable, everywhere it has been tried.

The masses may not be able to comprehend the theoretical argument of why Socialism cannot work (see Ludwig von Mises' masterpiece "Socialism"), but even dullards are capable of feeling pain. Experiential learning is more suited to mass education than theory. The ideals of Social Justice, Green Energy and other holy causes which sound so great are put into proper perspective when one is forced to deal with them. These ideals don't look so good when they affect one's ability to afford food, find a job or support one's family.

That is the gift that Obama has unwittingly bestowed upon the nation. He enabled the masses to experience the beginnings of Socialism up close and personal.

Immigrants who experienced the horrors of Socialism, such as East Europeans or Cubans, believe this nation has lost its mind going in this failed direction. Now even the dullards are beginning to comprehend that this stove is hot and you shouldn't jump on it.

Thank you, President Obama, for exposing Liberalism so glaringly. You provided the country a gift, if they will accept it. Rather than slowly cooking the people in the pot, you turned up the heat too quickly. If you have a legacy, that will be it.

Obama provided the same service to this country as did Ludwig von Mises. Obama's was an experiential approach that ensured that more people could understand it. In the space of a few years Obama taught much of the country the importance of freedom, liberty and limited government. His mistake was trying to remove these aspects of American life too quickly. No textbook has been able to teach that lesson as effectively.

As a result, the masses are beginning to awaken from their complacency. They sense something is wrong, even though they might not understand quite what it is.

Some are thankful for President Obama and what appears to be the destruction of the Progressive ideal. Over the last two years I predicted that Obama would soon be at war with Democrats (October 2010, January, 2010 and November 2009 are but three examples). In the November 2009 piece, it was stated:

> We have a Failed Presidency that cannot be retrieved. The dream cannot be rebuilt because there was never a foundation to begin with. It was all show and no substance. Yes, it created much excitement and (false) hope. But so did Elmer Gantry and James Jones. However, the image was akin to an old Hollywood set, all facade and no depth. Now the winds of reality are slowly and inexorably tearing the facade away.

> The politicians in Congress see these same signs and read the polls. At this point they are trying to decide what is least dangerous for their individual careers. For the Republicans that probably means pouring gasoline on ship Obama. For the Democrats, it is a more difficult problem. Ultimately, I believe they will abandon the rotting ship. Politicians of both parties are like rats; they are survivors. All politicians will take that course

which they believe gives them the best chance for individual survival. Loyalty be damned.

That has not happened yet, but we are closer to that point. Let the political games begin. Many Democrats, both voters and elected officials, are beginning to wish they had never heard of one Barack Hussein Obama. What appeared initially to be "The One" has, for many, more properly become "The None."

Behind the scenes, Democrats will be working furiously to get rid of this impostor. Andrew Breitbart[3] described it thusly:

> I predict a tectonic shift among American Jews and within the Democratic Party if Obama doesn't quietly retire. All the spinning in the world can't spin away the trend of Scott Brown, the Tea Party victory of November 2010, and now the Turner earthquake.
>
> Many Democrats are awakening to the reality that their party has been hijacked by a radicalism completely unfamiliar to their parent's and grandparent's Democratic Party.
>
> An internal, partisan civil war is now brewing in that party. What I think tonight is less important than what Joe Lieberman, Bill Clinton, Evan Bayh, and the rest of the former, and now defunct, reasonable wing of the Democratic Party is thinking tonight.

Engineering a solution that removes Obama from running in 2012 will be difficult for Democrats. But when their own survival is at stake, something strange and radical could occur.

---

[3]http://biggovernment.com/abreitbart/2011/09/13/after-turner-earthquake-in-weiner-district-democrats-civil-war-against-obama-begins/

Americans are suffering economically. The economic situation unfortunately will get worse before it improves, regardless of who is in office and what policies are implemented.

For political fanatics and Jimmy Carter fans, there has never been a better time. At some point, Republicans might be Obama's only friends. After all, he has done so much for them.

Addendum to Original

While editing posts and articles for this book, the reaction of Socialists to Ludwig von Mises' criticisms (which began in 1920) came to mind. Oskar Lange, a leading Socialist theoretician, could not refute Mises's contention regarding the economic calculation problem. So Lange changed his approach (which was also unworkable according to Mises).

In gratitude (likely with tongue deeply embedded in cheek) Lange suggested that a statue of Mises should be erected as a tribute from Socialists everywhere for "correcting" Lange's error and moving Socialism forward.

Fast forward to the present. Is a Mises-Lange moment replaying? Should a statue of Obama be erected by grateful free-market advocates for Obama's service in showing their superiority? Has anyone been more effective in showing why we need markets and not central planning to allocate resources than Barack Obama?

13 Too Many People Know Him

OCTOBER 12, 2011

The Obama Problem is simple to explain but impossible to solve. The problem is Obama himself, and most people not named Barack or Michele are beginning to understand that.

President Obama's political career is in free fall. He will not be re-elected. **[A very incorrect prediction, in retrospect.]** Many Democrats and media now understand that is a distinct possibility. Mere months ago it was considered an impossibility.

13.1 In The Beginning

Mr. Obama burst onto the political scene as a relatively unknown wunderkind. He could read a mean teleprompter and did so with fanfare at the 2004 Democrat Convention. He had good speech writers, an intelligent and disciplined campaign strategy, a carefully crafted biography and a highly-accommodating media. He was charismatic and eloquent. Joe Biden awkwardly described him as "the first mainstream African-American who is articulate and bright and clean and a nice-looking guy."

13.2 The Perfect Storm

The 2008 election was the political equivalent of "a perfect storm." Two factors were key to Obama's election:

1. **Americans were disgusted with Washington, especially George Bush.** The media anointed Obama as their man. They publicized his strengths and hid his weaknesses. They painted him as an outsider, someone who could bridge the gap between political parties and make Washington function. The media anointed Obama and threw Hillary Clinton overboard in the primary process.

2. **The Republicans chose a sure loser to run, the shopworn Washington-establishment figure Senator John McCain.** McCain offered nothing that had not already been rejected by the public. He was little more than an elderly George W. Bush who carried the additional baggage of a Washington insider. It is likely that any Democrat could have beaten McCain.

When the perfect storm cleared, Obama had been elected president.

13.3 Things Went Wrong Quickly

No president in recent history began his term with higher expectations and good will than Barack Obama. The promise and exhilaration that accompanied his election was short-lived. In less than three years, Obama plummeted from the heights (his "Messiah" arrival stage) to the depths (a candidate for the "worse than Jimmy Carter" award).

The turnaround was astonishing in speed and magnitude. To put matters in perspective, it took George Bush almost eight years to hit bottom. And, Bush had little support from the media, a force that continues to protect Obama.

To understand Obama's loss in popularity, it is necessary to recognize that he was a fluke. He was an unlikely candidate, pushed to his party's nomination as a result of the media. His election was a quirk, more aberration than achievement. It is not a strain to conclude that the mainstream media, rather than the electorate, put Obama into that position.

In hindsight, a great mistake was made. Even the fawning media and the Democrat establishment now recognize that, although are unwilling to publicly admit it. Their behavior is analogous to refusing to discuss a friend's terminal illness in the hope that it, or he, will somehow go away.

The media and the Democrat party are at risk if the tragedy they foisted off on the nation continues. Their future is intertwined with the Obama Problem. **Both sponsored him and both may ultimately be held accountable**. The battle so easily won in 2008 may cost them subsequent battles, perhaps the war itself.

Both institutions know the risk. They just have no easy way of solving the problem.

Opinions regarding factors responsible for Mr. Obama's political demise abound. A full menu is available: the economy, broken promises, cronyism, socialism, bailouts, corruption, disillusionment, inexperience, incompetence, duplicity, Chicago-style politics, etc. Pundits have a rich environment from which to select when they finally get around to autopsying the Obama presidency.

13.4 The Root Cause

The factors above are relevant but not primary. The central problem is that **there never was any substance to Obama**. He was the political equivalent of a Potemkin village. There was nothing behind the facade. There was no "there" there. All of the problems arise from this now-obvious and unfixable flaw.

President Obama is little more than a **run-of-the-mill Hollywood extra**, hired to play President of the United States. A brilliant marketing campaign, coupled with a perfect storm, put him in office. The marketing campaign was so good that it deserves a case study by the Harvard Business School.

The "man with no past" and the Hollywood veneer combined to make a perfect candidate. "Sizzle" rather than substance was sold. Little was known about Obama and his past, allowing David Axelrod to market the political equivalent of a Rorschach blot.

Voters saw in Obama whatever they desired. To some, he was a breath of fresh air, a man of principles. To others he was an outsider, not a crass politician. Others saw him as a chance to prove they were not racists. Still others saw him as the re-incarnation of Roosevelt or whoever else they admired.

Obama was a blank slate to be imagined or drawn by the voters. He was a chameleon which each voter could turn into whatever they envisioned as his ideal candidate. Voters created and bought a product that existed only in their minds. They elected Chauncey Gardiner[1]. Unfortunately their selection did not come with Peter Sellers' range or abilities.

A brilliant marketing strategy can make a first sale, but performance and satisfaction is required for the second. Axelrod's skill in marketing had no counterpart in production. **No one seemed to be concerned about delivering a product after it was sold.**

Obama entered office unorganized and unstructured. He knew nothing about management, organization or leadership. Nor did he bring in associates with these skills. As a result, this Hollywood mannequin was almost immediately exposed to those not blinded by the hype. The public had purchased a product that did not perform. Furthermore, the purchase had never operated in any environment comparable to the one it was intended.

Marketing can do many things, but it cannot sell a product that people have tried and rejected. That is Obama's re-election problem

[1]http://en.wikipedia.org/wiki/Being_There

– too many people have tried the product and know it doesn't perform.

The irony is that Mr. Obama has not changed. He is the same man who was elected the first time. His problem is not communicating, Republicans, George Bush, tsunamis or anything else. **His problem is the man in the mirror. There is no more there than an image.**

Obama was all hype. There was no underlying substance. That realization is dawning on voters and shows up in polls. Richard Nixon was never liked, but he was competent. Obama was liked but never competent.

The old phrase, **familiarity breeds contempt** likely explains Obama's drop in popularity better than more complicated explanations. People realized that the product they thought they bought was not the product they received.

Addendum:

Between the time this piece was submitted and its publication, an excellent article by James Taranto[2]appeared appeared that dealt with this same subject. Mr. Taranto is a skilled writer, so you probably should read his take on this subject. Here are a few excerpts from Mr. Taranto's article:

> Portnoy observes: "What I believe is happening is that the left is reading the handwriting on the wall and resigning itself to the harsh reality [that] the man they trusted to ˜fundamentally transform America' is on the verge of being unelected."

> Not only does Obama's re-election look to be in serious jeopardy, but his presidency has been an almost unmitigated disaster for progressive liberalism, nearly

---

[2]http://online.wsj.com/article/SB10001424052970203633104576625132698318672.html

every tenet of which has been revealed to be untenable either practically, politically or both.

The left got what it wanted in 2008: a liberal president with a sweeping agenda and big Democratic majorities capable of enacting it. The result has been a great and failed experiment in progressive politics and governance. In due course, one hopes, the left will absorb some lessons" but for now, they seem to be suffering a nervous breakdown.

14 Obama Will Not Win Re-election

MAY 30, 2012

It is time to call the 2012 election. President Obama cannot win. He will likely lose big, in a lopsided election. Pundits will claim to be surprised when the outcome becomes apparent. They should not be, as the signs of such a result seem everywhere, despite the mainstream media's attempts to suppress them.

Some reasons why Obama will lose are incompetence, lack of likability and duplicity. Obama has alienated many in the electorate, including large numbers who supported him the first time. In 2012 many of these supports may vote against him or just stay home.

14.1 How Did Obama Get Elected The First Time?

Barack Hussein Obama is a self-created myth, enhanced by David Axelrod and a compliant media. He is a chameleon who takes on whatever shape and form suits his purposes and goals. There is little substance behind the facade. He is the Elmer Gantry of American politics with all of the acting skills so envied by Hollywood. Obama is capable of assuming whatever shape, form, image or position that works to his advantage.

A few examples of his "flexibility:"

- He changed his name when he believed it served him to do so.

- He is not a religious man, but joined a Black Liberation Church to sell his *bona fides* to the black community in his early days in Chicago.
- He said that Preacher Jeremiah Wright was like his father, yet threw him under the bus when it became convenient (necessary).
- He claimed to have been born in Kenya in order to enhance book sales as a younger man.
- He likely lied on his applications to college to gain foreign student status. At the time that category provided more favorable admission and funding treatment than afforded domestic blacks.
- He claimed to be a Constitutional Law Professor when he was neither a professor nor particularly well-versed in the Constitution.

Little was known about Obama when he entered the primary campaign. As pointed out earlier[1]:

> Obama entered office as little more than a Rorschach blot. Much of his past had been hidden. What was known had been carefully scrubbed and scripted. His campaign avoided specifics. His speeches sounded great when delivered but were vacuous when read. Little defined him except what observers chose to imagine. He was a master in allowing you to believe whatever was most important to you.

His greatest asset was his "unknownness." As a blank slate, voters imagined whatever they most wanted. A clever marketing campaign enhanced their imagination.

The product was marketed in the following manner:

---

[1] http://www.economicnoise.com/?p=27579

As a political "newbie" and the first serious African-American candidate, he played well. He was an outsider who would clean up Washington. For many he was the great healer who would bring unity to Republicans and Democrats, blacks and whites and America and its enemies. His "Kumbayah"campaign was hailed by the media, and a large naive segment of the electorate believed it.

14.2 Why Obama Will Lose The Election

Understanding why Obama will lose this next election is less difficult than understanding how he won the first time. Barack Obama was a fluke, an unlikely candidate with no demonstrated experience in anything other than reading a teleprompter and sounding good,

He was pushed to his party's nomination by the media. His election was a quirk, rather than something truly earned. Any Democrat who gained the nomination was likely ensured the presidency. "Bush fatigue" and the hapless John McCain made that almost certain.

Obama will lose the next election because his greatest asset is gone. Voter imagination can no longer be manipulated. Facts are available. Obama now has a record and will not be re-elected because **too many people now know him**.

Buyer's remorse characterizes much of the electorate. What people got was nothing like what they were promised or expected. The blank slate is now a full blown portrait filled with failure, warts, scars and other imperfections.

Obama's track record is abysmal. Floyd and Mary Beth Brown[2] discussed four of Obama's failures:

---

[2]http://www.westernjournalism.com/stories-hear-obama/

- Obama's 825 billion dollar stimulus failed to keep unemployment below 8 percent as Obama promised. Since President Obama's stimulus passed, America has lost 1.1 million jobs. If you count people who have become discouraged and are no longer seeking jobs, some economists believe that the real unemployment rate is above twenty percent.

- Obama called his health care package one of his major accomplishments. He told CBS' Steve Kroft he was "putting in place a system in which we're going to start lowering health care costs." Yet it has failed to make health insurance more affordable. According to the fact watchdog website FactCheck.org, ObamaCare is actually making health care "less affordable." Workers paid an average of $132 more for family coverage just this year.

- Obama predicted his investments in green energy would create 5 million jobs, but the Wall Street Journal reports: "The green jobs subsidy story gets more embarrassing by the day. Three years ago President Obama promised that by the end of the decade, America would have five million green jobs, but so far, some $90 billion in government spending has delivered very few."

- Obama pledged to cut the deficit in half, saying: "And that's why today I'm pledging to cut the deficit we inherited by half by the end of my first term in office." Even if every part of Obama's deficit reduction proposal was enacted, the deficit at the end of his first term would still be $1.33 trillion, more than twice what he promised.

In an earlier article[3], other failures were highlighted:

- His Obamacare legislation, despite all the State propaganda supporting it, remains unpopular and is viewed by more than half the country as unconstitutional. Recent hearings in front of the Supreme Court were embarrassing to the Administration. The legislation is wildly over budget and threatens to accelerate the bankruptcy of the nation. Further, the more people begin to deal with its implementation the more unworkable it is considered and the more it is considered a mistake. Obama's trophy piece of legislation is increasingly viewed as an unworkable, unmitigated disaster.

- Relations between Republicans and Democrats and blacks and whites are worse than at any time in my lifetime. The former is on evidence every day. The latter was demonstrated by the circus surrounding the tragic death of Trayvon Martin.

- The country's foreign policy is a growing embarrassment. America has alienated many of its allies. America and its enemies are not doing so well either. We don't have a Cold War, although we don't need one with what is happening. Russia is not our ally. China is exerting its newly-developed muscle. Iran openly mocks the President as it proceeds to nuclear weaponry. North Korea plays Lucy with the football and Charlie Brown falls for the trick every time. The Mid-East is in shambles with the Asian Spring being

---

[3]http://www.economicnoise.com/?p=27579

nothing more than the replacement of tyrants who were friendly to the US with tyrants who are not. Israel looks like they will have to act alone against their existential threat.

- The economy has not improved despite record stimulus. Economic statistics are routinely "massaged" to make outcomes look better. Suffocating regulations, increasing debt levels and regime uncertainty prevent recovery. Capital and talent increasingly flee the US.

- Obama has mortgaged the country's future with his spending. By the time of the election he will have added almost $6 Trillion in new debt. There is no interest in cutting spending despite the doomsday warnings from multiple sources. Markets will eventually choose how and when the spending will cease.

- Gasoline prices are soaring. The so-called "green energy" initiative has been exposed as corrupt political payoffs that will not produce economic energy for decades, if ever. Coal is under attack, exploration for oil is unnecessarily restricted, pipelines are stymied and power plants are closing. Politically correct politics moves us away from modernity toward the Stone Age.

- Obama is no longer seen as The One, just another scheming Chicago politician. He is increasingly viewed as arrogant, dishonest and incompetent. These are not messianic-like attributes. He is just another politician, although more flawed than most.

The American voters made a terrible mistake in 2008. That mistake is now apparent, especially to political analysts. Nothing Obama promised has been accomplished. Furthermore, much of what he did, added new problems and exacerbated old ones.

Even the fawning media and the Democrat establishment recognize his failings, although neither is willing to publicly discuss them. Democrats should have replaced this deficient candidate long ago. It is too late now. Democrat sympathizers can only hope that this election does not destroy what remains of the Party.

Based on the debacle that was the 2010 election, that fear is not unfounded. If anything, the mistake that was Obama is better known today than it was two years ago.

James Taranto[4] pointed out the despair among Democrats and their PR arm, the national press. In an editorial he cited several examples of disillusionment. Howard Portnoy was quoted in the piece stating:

> What I believe is happening is that the left is reading the handwriting on the wall and resigning itself to the harsh reality [that] the man they trusted to 'fundamentally transform America' is on the verge of being defeated.

Mr. Taranto added his own thoughts to those of the generally liberal pundits:

> Not only does Obama's re-election look to be in serious jeopardy, but his presidency has been an almost unmitigated disaster for progressive liberalism, nearly every tenet of which has been revealed to be untenable either practically, politically or both.

[4]http://online.wsj.com/article/SB10001424052970203633104576625132698318672.html

14.3 Obama Stumbles Out of The Gate

Several different recent weeks have been described by various pundits as "Obama's worst week yet." The rate of decline appears to steepen as the campaign season heats up.

Now the Obama political campaign is seen as being in disarray. Politico[5] described the early stages of the campaign as follows:

> That's the unmistakable reality for Democrats since Obama officially launched his reelection campaign three weeks ago. Obama, not Mitt [6]Romney[7], is the one with the muddled message and the one who often comes across as baldly political. Obama, not Romney, is the one facing blow back from his own party on the central issue of the campaign so far Romney's history with Bain [8]Capital[9]. And most remarkably, Obama, not Romney, is the one falling behind in[10] fundraising[11].

Obama's campaign was run so smoothly four years ago that it likely created a false impression of Obama's campaigning abilities. This campaign cannot be run the same way for obvious reasons. Nor can it run smoothly. There is nothing Obama can run on that can be considered an achievement other than the over-hyped bin Laden killing.

Obama appears silly trying to blame Bush for the last four years. This approach is a blatant attempt to avoid responsibility for his own failures. Perhaps he should blame even earlier presidents for

---

[5]http://www.politico.com/news/stories/0512/76752.html#ixzz1vsV1ETH5
[6]http://politico.com/tag/MittRomney
[7]http://politico.com/tag/MittRomney
[8]http://www.politico.com/news/stories/0512/76602.html
[9]http://www.politico.com/news/stories/0512/76602.html
[10]http://www.politico.com/news/stories/0512/76556.html
[11]http://www.politico.com/news/stories/0512/76556.html

his woes. After all, Madison and Jefferson provided the Constitution which he considers a roadblock in his attempt to remake America.

14.4 A Bigger Democrat Problem

There is a bigger problem for Democrats than one election and one failed candidate. The strategy adopted long ago, and responsible for most of their success over the last eighty years, has played itself out.

Franklin Roosevelt, during the Great Depression, saw the value of buying votes by spreading benefits around. It was successful and a strategy refined by subsequent Democrats over the years. The strategy was based on identity politics and rewarding certain segments of the population with gifts in exchange for their votes.

It was a brilliant strategy for winning elections but hardly a strategy conducive to governance. As a result, the Democrat coalition today is a motley collection of interest groups with little in common other than "we want more." That makes it impossible to have a coherent governing strategy.

As an example of how governance becomes more difficult or even impossible, consider the budget. Democrats have not developed a budget for almost three years. Budgets are difficult in periods of declining government revenues. They are especially difficult when minority voter groups expect to be treated better every year. Showing which interest groups benefit at the expense of the others is a problem they do not want to address.

As the country approaches its Thatcher point, there is less money to buy votes. Goodies will eventually be taken away. This situation has serious implications for both political parties, but especially the Democrats.

The Democrat Party now exists and survives based on one simple strategy – **making dependency more attractive.**

It has become the party of plunder, taking from the productive and giving to the unproductive to buy enough votes to remain relevant.

The Democrat Party approaches this election with an ogre driving an empty ice cream truck. They will lose the election and many more unless they redefine themselves in terms of something other than Santa Claus. Sadly, for Democrats (and many= Republicans) Santa died. Strategies that worked when he was alive need to be re-drawn.

14.5 Qualification

My projection of Obama's defeat is based on some semblance of sanity among the electorate. H. L. Mencken might consider that a dangerous assumption, but I am hopeful.

If Obama wins, get the hell out of Dodge! **Even if the election is close and Obama loses, leave if you are less than fifty years old and have ambition and ability. If the election is even close, the country is lost!**

> [H.L. Mencken was a very wise man. My prediction overestimated the wisdom of voters. Obama was re-elected. Get out of Dodge!]

15 The Next Election Could Be Fatal

SEPTEMBER 17, 2012

For the last thirty or so years, every election has been termed "the most important election in history" or described in similar hyperbole. Outcomes of elections are important, but few are "game-changers" as pundits routinely claim.

For the first time in my life, the next election will truly fit this exaggerated billing. **This election is truly the most important one in history.** So too will the one after that and on into the future.

15.1 An Inflection Point

The United States of America is at an inflection point. The outcome of this election will determine whether we continue to veer off-course or return to a conventional trajectory.

The issue is whether we continue to reinvent this country in ways that have failed everywhere or return to the traditions, values and outcomes that have been the envy of the world. That is the choice!

The key figure in this choice is Barack Obama. What he represents and insists on imposing is a revolution in values, markets and what has been known as the American way of life. His opponent, Mitt Romney, hardly seems ideological enough to combat this direct assault on liberty.

Romney seems a good and decent man, one that you might admire as a competent and fair boss. He does not convey the intensity of political mission as his opponent. Competency would be welcome, but it is not sufficient. Soviet bureaucrats were competent as they administered to unproductive tasks. Competency in pursuit of wrong goals is a liability rather than an asset. Incompetency in pursuit of wrong goals is what the country currently has. Unfortunately that is also a liability, just not as big a one.

The intensity of the bases of the two parties does not appear equal. Obama-detesters exist who didn't before. Most came to this position concluding one of the following described Obama: 1) the man is incompetent and made matters worse; or, 2) he is out to destroy what was America.

Anti-Obama feeling is strong and represents a larger minority of the opposing party than it did four years ago. Still it does not come close to matching the core of dependency voters who view each election in terms of life and death (or living well versus living). This intense core far outnumbers the Obama-detesters.

15.2 The Issue

It is difficult to properly express the importance of this election without sounding overly political or alarmist. David Solway[1] achieves a balance in his description of what is at stake:

> The United States of America is now something alarmingly close to what we might describe as the rogue regime of Obamerica. The "end," in the acceptation of "purpose," of this strange new nation appears to be the reversal or erasure of its Republican heritage and its replacement by what Barry Rubin calls a stealth-leftist[2] anti-American substitute.

---

[1]http://pjmedia.com/website/the-end-of-obamerica/
[2]http://pjmedia.com/barryrubin/2012/09/10/barack-obama-is-a-dangerous-leftist-of-a-new-kind-not-a-communist-muslim-marxist-or-socialist/

The projected "end" of Obamerica would seem to be nothing less than the material end of America as we have known it throughout its storied history. Its free-market economy is currently in tatters, its competitive edge and productivity blunted by a meretricious "stimulus" and by redistributionist economics, its Triple A credit rating downgraded amid concerns about the government's budget deficit and rising debt burden, and its unemployment numbers beyond acceptable. Racial and ethnic divisions have been exacerbated by the president's incendiary rhetoric.

Owing to Obama's policies, America's network of reliable alliances is in disarray as the program of appeasement and rapprochement with its adversaries grows ever more emphatic. At the same time the power and authority of the erstwhile "leader of the free world" has started demonstrably to wane. And if Obama has his way and is re-elected, he will enjoy, as he confided[3] to former Russian President Dmitri Medvedev, even more "flexibility" to pursue his ends.

The looming choice for the U.S. on November 6 of this year is stark and unforgiving. The re-election of Barack Obama will mean the "end," in its terminal sense, of the America of yore, of the constitutional republic on which the West has grudgingly depended for its defense and prosperity and whose citizens were once the envy of an ungrateful world. An unprecedented experiment in free market economics and individual liberty will have fallen victim to an unscrupulous agenda that intends its demise. Only the end of Obamerica can

[3]http://www.reuters.com/article/2012/03/26/us-nuclear-summit-obama-medvedev-idUSBRE82P0JI20120326

prevent the nation's decline. History is about to be made or unmade.

A victory for Obamerica can come only at the expense of America itself, and a heretofore undefeated nation will go down to the first and greatest and quite possibly lasting defeat in the chronicle of its tenure.

This is what is at stake and what American voters will soon determine. Will it be Obamerica or will it be America? May they choose wisely.

It is frightening that one election can have such importance to a country. But that is what is now at stake for America.

15.3 Elections Were Never Intended To Be Life-Changing

The Founders never intended an election to be so important. The Constitution was designed to keep government small, unobtrusive and unimportant. The role of government was limited to prevent it from increasing power and importance.

The primary purpose of government was to provide defense against external enemies and protect property rights. These services were established as public functions on the assumption that they could be provided more efficiently publicly rather than privately.

The Leviathan that government has become was never intended. Its current size, power and responsibilities contradict both the intent and the black letter law of the Founders. If the Founders could see what their efforts spawned, they might conclude that living under King George was a better way of life than what we evolved to. "Taxation without representation" seems better than the taxation with representation that we have. It is hard to imagine things being worse, although we appear headed to just such a place.

No election was intended to have the potential to change the framework of the country. That framework was intended to be sacrosanct, outside of the reach of politics and majority rule. Yet that is no longer the case and every election now poses such a threat.

This condition was not created by Mr. Obama. Two hundred years of political meddling emasculated the Constitution and brought us to this point. The Constitution came under attack because it prevented political figures from imposing their views upon the citizenry. Power-hungry politicians and rent-seeking voters were present from the beginning and eventually triumphed over the Constitution.

Two hundred years of tinkering and political meddling has reduced the Constitution to little more than a quaint historical artifact. The Rule of Man has now, *de facto*, replaced The Rule of Law.

15.4 The New Consequence of Elections

Elections, designed to be rather meaningless events, suddenly have become the most important things in many peoples' lives. The dependency class has a vested interest in whoever promises them a better standard of living. This constituency has no "skin in the game" so generally votes for the one who promises them more.

Both political parties have pursued these zombie voters, ensuring increases in their numbers and importance. Today they represent almost 50% of the electorate. The late Milton Friedman pointed to 50% as the tipping point for a democratic society. Once reached, he thought no political solution could reverse the process.

The Economic Problem

Barack Obama represents an existential threat to the American way of life. His re-election means America will be changed in the wrong direction. Electing Mitt Romney might delay this outcome. Ronald Reagan merely slowed the decline and Mitt Romney does not appear to be Ronald Reagan.

If Obama is defeated, and I expect he will be, Romney's economic policies will be better than Obama's. The President's so-called economic plan never amounted to more than the hot air of hope and change and payoffs to political friends. The economic hole is deep and will be difficult to overcome, even with proper policies. An economic recovery is necessary but does not solve the real problem facing the country.

The Real Problem

The underlying and seemingly unsolvable problem is the emasculation of the Constitution. That enabled the Rule of Man to trump the Rule of Law. That seemingly simple change is the root cause of our economic and other problems. Government has become too large, too powerful and too intrusive.

Divisions in the country have never been greater. Racial and income divides are especially harmful. Cronyism is rampant. All of these come about by government taking on tasks it was never intended to do.

The most important dichotomy is the dependent versus productive divide. The Democrat Party played the dependency game to its advantage. That is why, despite the worst economic and foreign policy conditions in eighty years, this election is still considered too close to call.

Barack Obama is an incompetent ideologue. Hopefully he will be defeated and the near loss of the American way of life will shock people back to their senses.

Defeating Barack Obama does not solve the problem. The role of government must be returned to its Constitutional roots. History shows that lawmakers never relinquish power willingly.

Unless government can be re-caged, **we will always be one election away from disaster**. Defeating Obama buys time, but solves nothing. It pushes the problem off one election. At some point the American people will choose incorrectly and their way of life will be gone.

Democracy always destroys itself.

16 How Can The Election Be Close?

NOVEMBER 5, 2012

The election is tomorrow. The build up to this point has been somewhat surreal. Pollsters tell us that the election is too close to call, but that does not seem to coincide with logic or anecdotal evidence.

It is easy to distort reality based on pre-dispositions and desires. I have no interest in Romney winning other than he is not Obama. I am not a Republican, although generally believe their ideas are usually less bad than those of Democrats. I am what you might term an **"equal opportunity disliker" with respect to politics and politicians**.

I don't want to be ruled by either party, or anyone else for that matter.

16.1 Pre-Election Logic

Why does it seem impossible to call this race? My eyes tell me things that pollsters either don't see or people are unwilling to tell them. Here are a few reasons why Obama should lose:

- The country is stuck in a recession which Obama has made worse. After four years he still has no viable plan to remedy economic problems.
- Foreign policy, arguably less understandable to voters, is disintegrating. Benghazi is exploding all over Obama and is something he is unable to blame on someone else.

- More people are on food stamps and welfare than ever before. People sense that Obama is not displeased with this condition.
- Incomes are falling and unemployment is not. College graduates cannot get jobs commensurate with their education. Despair is growing.
- Median Net Worth is falling and prices are rising. The Middle Class standard of living has declined for four straight years.
- Retirement is no longer an option for large segments of the population.

These should be obvious conditions which people see and feel. They should be reflected in the vote.

Facts matter, especially to those concerned about the country, their future and the futures of their grandchildren. The electorate may not be the brightest, as H. L. Mencken always insisted. But they do feel pain and do not relish it. Cats who jump on a hot stove are smart enough never to jump on any stove again. **Is the US electorate dumber than a cat?**

The so-called parasite class (dependents living at the expense of others) understand what is in their best interest and will vote for whoever promises to extend their benefits. That would be Obama. Yet this so-called parasite class is a smaller sub-set of the broader class of those receiving government assistance. Conflating the two often leads to overstating the importance of the dependency class.

Many on government assistance are there not by choice but by circumstance. Some have never been in this position before. They want a job again, where they can have a purpose, a role and respect. Many who paid into the social insurance program understand it is not sustainable. They will vote to protect what they have, but it is difficult to determine what that means. Do they go to Obama who promises to protect all government spending? Or do many of them go to Republicans on the basis that other spending will be cut in order to protect their benefits?

It doesn't seem that this election should be close. The country is not that far gone! Barack Obama has surpassed Jimmy Carter as the worst president anyone alive has seen. Only the Kool-Aid drinkers and the infatuated mainstream media do not, or pretend to not, understand that.

There is likely not one person who voted for John McCain last time who will switch his vote to Obama this time. Disallusioned Obama supporters will switch. Republicans who stayed home four years ago rather than vote for McCain are not going to stay home again. [That turned out not to be true] Many will vote against Obama rather than for Romney.

16.2 Anecdotal Evidence

Crowd comparisons between Romney and Obama events suggest Obama is "old news." There are large crowds, energy and enthusiasm at the Romney events. There are small crowds and lack of enthusiasm at the Obama events.

Early voting suggests a strong turnout for Romney, at least when compared to the corresponding numbers four years ago. Women are breaking toward Romney. States that were never thought to be in play by pollsters suddenly look like they might be up for grabs – Pennsylvania and Michigan are two. Momentum seems to be moving away from Obama.

Newspaper endorsements reflect the mood of their readers and reinforce the trends above. The Des Moines *Register* endorsed Romney. Ditto the NY Daily News and many other papers who routinely endorse Democrats. Ben Shapiro[1] reports:

---

[1] http://www.breitbart.com/Big-Journalism/2012/11/04/11-papers-switch-to-Romney-1-to-Obama

> According to the University of California, Santa Barbara American Presidency Project study[2] of the top 100 newspaper editorial endorsements, Mitt Romney has seen a vast wave of switches from 2008 Obama endorsers. Obama, meanwhile, has seen only one newspaper that endorsed John McCain come around to endorse him. At the same time, many newspapers have also switched from Obama to "no endorsement."

There is not one constituency that reasonably can be seen increasing its support for Obama. Hard-core Democrat groups are uninspired. Turnout among them will be lower. Obama will win these groups by overwhelming majorities, but the groups may be smaller this time around.

Doug Ross[3] presented some interesting statistics that support the above. A survey commissioned by the Washington Post is the source of his numbers. Mr. Ross' summary included the following (my emboldening):

> Overall, the Post-ABC poll found that **13 percent of 2008 Obama voters have decided to back Mitt Romney**.

Michael Barone[4] has predicted that Romney will win big (315 electoral votes). I agree with Mr. Barone, although have no feel for the number of electoral votes.

Ross, Barone and other obvious signs point to a Romney win, probably a big one.

---

[2] http://www.presidency.ucsb.edu/data/2012_newspaper_endorsements.php

[3] http://directorblue.websitespot.com/2012/11/chart-obama-defectors-and-what-they-mean.html

[4] http://www.powerlinewebsite.com/archives/2012/11/michael-barone-calls-it-for-romney.php

[Apparently I and many other people were the Kool-Aid imbibers. Obama won re-election rather easily. Another Dewey-Truman moment, or was all of this merely wishful thinking?

In any case, the dumb cat did jump back on the stove.]

17 Obama's Election Seals Our Fate

NOVEMBER 8, 2012

The Obama re-election dooms the country. It ensures that his ideology will be further imposed on the country.

His election means the continuing shift away from the Rule of Law, property rights, free men and free markets. Obama's vision of how the world works ensures a dire economy until an economic collapse resets everything. The rest of the world, apparently bigger Obama supporters than US voters, will not be immune from the consequences.

17.1 The Fundamentals of Progress

Peace and progress are the children of freedom. The wealth of nations was explained more than two hundred years ago by Adam Smith. Property rights and markets coordinate behavior in a manner in which all are made better off by the pursuit of self-interest.

President Obama's view of the world is in contradiction to anything that has ever succeeded. He believes elites should manage and direct people's lives. This "fatal conceit," as Friedrich Hayek called it, yields failure and misery wherever it is tried.

Ludwig von Mises pointed out that the progress of the West was achieved on a simple idea:

> The essential characteristic of Western civilization that distinguishes it from the arrested and petrified civiliza-

tions of the East was and is its concern for freedom
from the state.

Civilization advanced and prospered on the foundation of private
property, defined rights, free men, free markets and the Rule of Law.

Obama's approach is hostile to each of these pillars of progress.
It conflicts with the evidence of hundreds, nay, thousands, of years.
Obama's way has never produced prosperity. It always results in
impoverishment, unhappiness and unfulfilled lives. And those are
its lesser flaws.

There is no evidence of a country which abandoned the principles of
freedom and free markets ever returning via the political process.
Those who gain power never willingly relinquish it. Ludwig von
Mises observed:

> Political ideas that have dominated the public mind for
> decades cannot be refuted through rational arguments.
> They must run their course in life and cannot collapse
> otherwise than in great catastrophe.

The recent election was a prime example of how reason rarely
overcomes ideology. The masses are unable or unwilling to process complex logical argument. Unthinking enthusiasm for popular
ideas is much easier.

As a result, the country re-elected a man who does not believe in
American values or the principles necessary for progress and well-
being. His re-election occurred despite the worst record of domestic
and foreign policy of anyone in the last seven decades. In other
words, the American people re-elected a proven failure!

17.2 Where We Are Headed

The United States and Europe abandoned the fundamentals necessary for progress. Both are committed to the failed ideas of

Socialism. Both are on their own "roads to serfdom" and headed for catastrophe. Their economies will under perform. Remaining on this path ensures they will eventually collapse.

A potential economic dark age lies ahead. Standards of living will decline. Societies and civilizations will be at risk. Whatever remains of the myth that that tomorrow will always be better than today will be shattered. Time can and will run back. Progress can reverse.

Voluntary cooperation is being replaced by coercion and division. Segments of society are set off against each other. Civilization regresses toward a Hobbesian world:

> Whatsoever therefore is consequent to a time of Warre, where every man is Enemy to every man; the same is consequent to the time, wherein men live without other security, than what their own strength, and their own invention shall furnish them withall. In such condition, there is no place for Industry; because the fruit thereof is uncertain; and consequently no Culture of the Earth; no Navigation, nor use of the commodities that may be imported by Sea; no commodious Building; no Instruments of moving, and removing such things as require much force; no Knowledge of the face of the Earth; no account of Time; no Arts; no Letters; no Society; and which is worst of all, continuall feare, and danger of violent death; And the life of man, solitary, poore, nasty, brutish, and short.

Western civilization, once the shining city on the hill, has been tarnished. Countries have abandoned the principles that made them great and have lost much of their luster. The world may soon be without a beacon of freedom and success.

17.3 The Implications

The mathematics of the debt situation were intractable before the election. Someone committed to solving this problem would likely fail because the debt burden is so large. That assumption will not be tested because Obama has no intention of dealing with this issue.

A collapse now appears inevitable. Government spending will not shrink. Deficits will rise. Taxes will rise. Economic activity will fall. The debt death spiral will accelerate and strangle what economic activity remains. Ultimately economies will implode. Societies and economies will be sucked into the abyss.

Obama had no viable economic plan for the last four years. He is still without one. There has been no progress economically. Instead, valuable time and resources were squandered (government debt rose $5 Trillion during this period with nothing to show for it except its crippling future effects). Government spending will continue for the next four years. It will not work, but it is all that Obama knows. It may be a way to continue to hide the cancer that afflicts economies and societies.

This election accelerated the speed toward collapse. Higher government spending and more Federal Reserve money will not alter the destination. They only aid the devastation. **We are now on the super highway to RUIN.**

18 How To Win Elections: Make Zombies

NOVEMBER 8, 2012

In light of Obama's re-election, the topic of zombies (a popular one judging by the number of TV shows featuring them) as a political tool deserves some comment.

18.1 What Is A Zombie?

"Zombies" are voters who are also government dependents. They cast votes on the basis of who is expected to provide them the most goodies.

For a zombie, there is no need to know issues, plans or programs. All that matters is knowing which candidate will keep your benefits coming and preferably growing. That candidate usually has a "D" immediately after his name. Those with "R"s after their names are not unfamiliar with this vote-buying nor averse to using similar tactics. They just don't do it as well or as recklessly if you prefer.

Apparently our government has succeeded in making almost half of the population dependent upon it. This number overstates the problem in that it includes Social Security recipients, most of whom are merely collecting returns they paid for. On the other hand it does not include government workers. They are not "dependents" in the sense that they are paid (overpaid) for work they perform. However, all benefit from a growing government and have similar incentives in that regard to zombies.

Phil Izzo in the WSJ[1] discussed a paper from the National Bureau of Economic Research[2]. The results will shock many people. It doesn't focus on zombies but it clearly shows how close to the edge many are living. Here are some of the findings:

The survey asked a simple question:

> "If you were to face a $2,000 unexpected expense in the next month, how would you get the funds you need?"

In the U.S., 24.9% of respondents reported being certainly able, 25.1% probably able, 22.2% probably unable and 27.9% certainly unable. The $2,000 figure

> "reflects the order of magnitude of the cost of an unanticipated major car repair, a large copayment on a medical expense, legal expenses, or a home repair," the authors write. On a more concrete basis, the authors cite $2,000 as the cost of an auto transmission replacement and research that reported low-income families claim to need about $1500 in savings for emergencies.

18.2 Destroying Lives

These statistics are shocking and shameful. Government policies have made people poorer and encouraged them to live beyond their means. Many of these people have been conditioned to have no

---

[1]http://websites.wsj.com/economics/2011/05/23/nearly-half-of-americans-are-financially-fragile/

[2]http://papers.nber.org/papers/w17072

sense of personal responsibility, believing that someone will take care of them. The idea of having a "nest egg," planning for the future or having some funds for a "rainy day" appears to have been erased from many people's DNA. Many of these people are not economic zombies – yet. The manner in which they have been encouraged to live, however, makes them behave in a similar matter. If/when they finally get pushed over the line, they will to government for help. Most probably vote Democrat today. More will tomorrow.

The paragraph above is harsh. Not all people with no or little savings fit into this category, at least on a permanent basis. Some are victims of circumstances resulting from the bad economy or misfortune. Yet too many have adopted a lifestyle unfamiliar with work, work habits, thrift or self-improvement. For many, it is all they know or have ever known. Normal aspirations are destroyed by perverse welfare incentives and the belief that there is a safety net for which they can qualify whenever needed.

Given the incentives, such behavior is understandable and may even be considered rational. If you attend government schools and come out with no education, it may not be possible to work. Skills may not be sufficient to command the minimum wage, a barrier erected by government that hurts those it claims to help.

The minimum wage makes it illegal for employers to hire folks at a lower wage, even though that reflects their value in terms of skills. Even if both parties agree that the transaction is satisfactory, it cannot occur because of the threat of legal penalties. This law prevents people with low skills from getting on the escalator of work, where better skills (and higher remuneration) can be obtained.

The welfare system itself often makes it economically irrational to work. Benefits may exceed the pay a person can obtain. Under such conditions, getting a job means taking a "pay cut." Unskilled people are unskilled. They are not necessarily irrational or stupid. They respond to incentives and disincentives the way the rest of us do.

Both the minimum wage and high welfare benefits tend to lock people into dependency. Benjamin Franklin understood that:

> I am for doing good to the poor, but I differ in opinion
> of the means. I think the best way of doing good to the
> poor, is not making them easy in poverty, but leading
> or driving them out of it. In my youth I traveled much,
> and I observed in different countries, that the more
> public provisions were made for the poor, the less they
> provided for themselves, and of course became poorer.
> And, on the contrary, the less was done for them, the
> more they did for themselves, and became richer.

When a government check exceeds what you can make working 40
hours a week (or even approximates it), is it rational to go to work?
Not if you grew up in a culture where the dole was acceptable. Even
those who didn't, are being asked to forgo immediate gratification
for future gratification (when skills increase and wages do also).
That is not something that many in today's instant gratification
society understand or believe they should be subjected to.

The people who succumb to the siren song of dependency represent
a tragedy, a stain on the country. They become hollow human
beings without goals or objectives other than today's gratification.
How many could develop into successful and admired individuals
if they were not encouraged to do otherwise? How many doctors,
teachers or scientific discoveries might otherwise have occurred had
these people chosen a different path? What is the opportunity cost
of ruining this talent pool?

**What should the penalty be for ruining the life of a fellow
human being?** The ultimate effects of doing so, in some respects,
are not very different from that of murder. But, instead of punishing
the criminals who commit these crimes, we **send them back to
Washington to create more zombies (or commit more murders
if you prefer)!**

Intellectuals believe they are much smarter than kite-flying Ben Franklin. They have a "better way." No idea, no matter how asinine, is considered good enough to be tried on an unsuspecting public. To the elite, the rest of the country exists as guinea pigs to be used for their noble social experiments.

18.3 The Failure of Welfare

The so-called War on Poverty has cost trillions of dollars. Edgar Browning[3] estimated the costs in 2005 to be in excess of $1 Trillion:

> Americans transfer more than a trillion dollars each year to low-income families through a bewildering variety of programs, all in the name of fighting poverty and inequality. That's about seven times the cost of the Iraq war.

In another article, Browning[4] put the 2005 spending level into perspective:

> To put a trillion dollars in perspective, it's more than twice our total spending on national defense.
>
> It's larger than the total revenue collected by the federal individual income tax.
>
> It's about ten times as much as we spent on redistributive policies in the 1950s (in inflation-adjusted dollars).

---

[3]http://www.brookesnews.com/081509welfarepoverty.html

[4]http://righttruth.typepad.com/right_truth/2008/09/war-on-poverty-the-high-costs-and-the-depressing-results.html

It's equal to the total before-tax cash income of middle-income households. That's right, we transfer to the low-income population an amount equal to the entire income of middle-income households, that is, households in the middle fifth (40th to 60th percentile) of the American income distribution.

Browning then put the matter into a different perspective, one that most can relate to:

If a trillion dollars were simply given to those counted as poor by the federal government (37 million in 2005), it would amount to $27,000 per person. That's $81,000 for a family of three, higher than the median income of all American families, and far greater than the poverty threshold of $15,577.

The costs of the poverty programs have only escalated since 2005. So has the waste as measured in unfulfilled human lives and potential.

What do we have to show for all this? As is typical of most government programs, the outcome was exactly opposite from the stated objectives. Poverty increased just as Ben Franklin knew it must. Enormous amounts of the country's resources were wasted that could have gone into economic advancements. Human lives were destroyed while increasing the poverty rate and establishing a permanent underclass of economic zombies.

The true cost of these programs is much greater than can be measured in money. The cost in wasted or misdirected lives is substantially greater, more tragic and disgraceful.

For Socialists, this damage is considered compassion. What the results are matter little. It is the intentions that are important. The road to hell is paved with intentions like these!

Some proponents of this madness never had good intentions. They recognized the personal benefits of creating economic dependents. In the minds of these power-crazed politicians, their election was more important than the damage they caused getting there. "To make an omelet some eggs must be broken." That includes eggs that we call human beings.

18.4 Doomed To Fail

Whether creating zombies or dependents was for compassionate or political purposes is irrelevant in the end. Eventually the system collapses under its own weight.

This observation from Ludwig von Mises should be taken seriously:

> A society that chooses between capitalism and socialism does not choose between two social systems; it chooses between social cooperation and the disintegration of society. Socialism is not an alternative to capitalism; it is an alternative to any system under which men can live as human beings.

The developing underclass that results from Socialism is now an intractable problem. It will grow worse unless we change direction. Sadly, it is difficult to imagine politicians addressing this issue. Doing so could mean the end of their tenure in the trough.

Instead, these political slave masters have the incentive to ruin even more lives so long as they can harvest votes from their efforts.

At some point, the entire system collapses from government promises piled on the backs of the productive. The time, place and painful circumstances for ending this horrible system is coming. The ending will not be controlled by political considerations but by limited resources and the reduction in rewards to productive effort.

III THE DECLINE CONTINUES

This part of the book provides coverage of events after Obama's 2012 re-election.

Obama was in a quasi lame-duck position after the 2010 mid-term rout. His re-election in 2012 put him into official lame-duck position. The House continued to be controlled by Republicans and Democrats continued to control the Senate. Gridlock was assured.

The 2014 mid-terms loom large for Obama's future. As this book went to press (about mid-year 2014), little has changed with respect to the condition of the country, the economy and foreign policy. Some of these areas have arguably worsened.

At this point it appears as though Republicans might take control of the Senate. Should that happen, Obama's agenda will move from lame to dead duck status.

If Obama has neither house of Congress under his control, matters could become more dangerous for the Administration and its allies. Impeachment becomes an outside possibility, given the potential for one or more of the alleged scandals to break open. That possibility is considered in Part Four.

In this section, the ObamaCare chapters were grouped together, slightly out of chronological order, because of their relationship with one another.

19 Obama's Pretense Is Over

NOVEMBER 8, 2013

In the beginning no one knew Barack Hussein Obama. His popularity was unsurpassed. Now that he is known, his popularity is at a low point (but it was high enough to beat Mitt Romney).

After nearly five years in office, Obama is no longer a blank slate and his magic is gone. Most now see that he was never what they imagined or wanted him to be.

Obama's style, once considered magical, is now seen as stilted and pompous. His regal presence has grown old and tiresome. Sans TOTUS, his teleprompter, the man seems unable to communicate any better than your next door neighbor.

That was image. Substance was judged even harsher. Campaign promises were not kept. Managerial ability never existed either in Obama or his staff. Hot air seemed to be the only product this Administration could produce.

People penetrated the mist that once enveloped and protected Obama. Behind the facade they discovered a mean-spirited, arrogant, lying incompetent. He was the Wizard of Oz without any of the charm.

David Limbaugh[1] summed up Obama:

> At the beginning, people could argue that Obama would usher in a period of prosperity and bipartisanship and that things would get better in America.

---

[1] http://www.davidlimbaugh.com/mt/archives/2013/11/column_obamacar_3.html

But after five years of unconscionably reckless federal spending, a wholesale assault on our domestic energy industries, endless abuses of executive authority and other lawless incursions on the Constitution, unprecedented divisiveness and polarization across economic, racial and gender lines, America's declining power and prestige in the world, an explosion of the welfare state and the worst economic recovery in 60 years, how can anyone who cares about this nation's future and the well-being of our children and grandchildren keep supporting this man's policies? Read more[2]

Familiarity has not served Obama well. When Obama's curtain was pulled back, incompetence, deviousness and meanness were found. Integrity, leadership and competence, qualities Americans expect in their presidents, were conspicuously missing. The marketing gimmickry that propelled Obama to the highest office in the land had expired.

Many finally saw the real Obama. He was no messiah nor was he the "One We Are Waiting For." He turned out to be just another politician, although seemingly more oriented to maintaining his popularity than serving the country. A recent Gallup poll found his approval rating below 40%, a ranking lower than George W. Bush at the same time in his presidency.

Obama's popularity seemed inversely related to how well people knew him. Hollywood might describe the phenomenon of Barack Obama as "without legs." That is the term applied to movies that open strong but have no follow through. Word of mouth is generally what takes movies "legs" away. For Obama, the same phenomenon seemed to be in play – **familiarity seems to have bred contempt.**

Heroes fall further than regular men, especially when they are seen

---

[2]http://www.wnd.com/2013/11/obamacare-is-obama-unmasked/
#ZPd7IOZviQYPKy9U.99

to have been phony from the start. Americans do not like to be "conned."

Will Obama try to continue his act, now seen through by all but the most mind-numbed followers? Or will he abandon any pretense of heroism and take on the bad guy role? It would appear that he has little choice. There is no way to return to the act that got him elected and re-elected.

20 Scorecard For The ObamaCare Debacle

NOVEMBER 11, 2013

The debacle known as ObamaCare continues to haunt Democrats and hurt Americans.

The game isn't over, but early returns are nonexistent, at least if you count actual enrollees. The system is an unmitigated disaster, destined to make medical care and insurance costs worse. The full magnitude of these effects have not yet been felt.

The health care website, bearing the brunt of the criticism, is unlikely to be fixed by the end of this month. In hindsight, it will probably be seen as one of the lesser problems with the program. When the true costs and effects on doctors and patients are known, the inability to sign up may, in hindsight, be considered one of the positive features of the plan.

20.1 What Were They Thinking?

ObamaCare had little hope of gaining popular support. A health care system in which 80% of participants were happy, provided a real world example of why the folksy advice – "if it ain't broke, don't fix it" – should be heeded. Politicians with favorability ratings in the teens believed they could take away a product with 80% approval. Political ideology apparently supercharges normal levels of stupidity.

Few independent observers believe that the "fixin" was an improvement. The Rube Goldberg system will eventually work in some fashion, but it will never work as well as what ObamaCare demolished.

A minority may eventually benefit by obtaining some type of insurance where they had none before. Most people, however, will be made worse off incurring higher premiums and deductibles and fewer options for medical care. Medical quality will deteriorate and rationing will occur.

A fundamental truth, that all governments refuse to accept, is on display with this legislation. Voluntary exchange always improves the position of both parties engaged in the trade or it would not take place. Consumer and producer are made better off. That was, at least partially, the basis for health care in this country. [Government intervention had destroyed much of the market prior to the passage of ObamaCare.]

ObamaCare removes much of the choice from the system. Any time choice is reduced people are made worse off. In the case of ObamaCare, not only options have been removed, coercion and central command has been introduced. The mandates and penalties exist because the product offered cannot stand on its own. People must be forced into buying this sub-standard product.

20.2 Frankenstein Monster

Government has imposed its version of a "better" system. The Statist plan is a Frankenstein monster, designed by central planners who "know" what is best for the rest of us. This hubris has succeeded in making almost everyone unhappy.

Most government projects end up producing consequences the opposite of the announced purposes. The overused phrase "unintended consequences" exists as a result of Statist planners. The phrase is little more than a euphemism for "Socialism never works" or "government does nothing well."

Millions have had their insurance canceled. Few desire or are able to sign up on the dysfunctional website. Most are shocked to learn that their new policies will be more expensive and less comprehensive.

Coercion is no substitute for freedom, yet it is the basis of every government rule or law. Consumers lose whenever government gets involved. Producers (insurance companies) will likely lose in the future as the central planners move toward their goal of a single payer system.

The best health care system in the world is crumbling as a result of this ideologically-motivated travesty.

John Nolte[1] provides a description of what we know so far (most emboldening added):

> **New Gallup poll**[2] brings more terrible news for President Obama and his signature health plan, showing that only 22% of uninsured Americans intend to buy insurance through the ObamaCare exchanges.
>
> One of the major selling points for using ObamaCare to disrupt our health care system (that polls showed **up to 80% of Americans were satisfied** with) was to insure the uninsured. But according to this poll, **only a very small minority of that small minority is even interested in obtaining insurance.**
>
> Even more troubling is the realization that a month ago, that number was double; a full 44% of the uninsured said they would purchase insurance though the exchanges. Over the course of a month, however, the reality of ObamaCare scared off half of that 44%. The

[1]http://www.breitbart.com/Big-Government/2013/11/08/poll-78-percent-of-uninsured-not-interested-in-obamacare

[2]http://www.gallup.com/poll/165776/uninsured-americans-ignoring-health-exchange-sites.aspx

high cost of premiums, the high deductibles customers have to pay regardless of any tax subsidy, and the unforgivable bungling of the rollout only discouraged those who we blew up a perfectly good health care system to help.

The worse news is that you can bet that the 22% who do intend to sign up are made up of the oldest and sickest among the uninsured. Meanwhile, the 78% who are uninterested in being insured are likely the youngest and healthiest. This means a sicker and older pool of enrollees, which means **higher premiums for a couple hundred million Americans who were perfectly satisfied with what they had,** that is, before President Obama, Democrats, and the media decided what was best for us.

As of now, the poll shows only 18% of the uninsured have even tried to visit a marketplace website. When you look at the nearly 4 million Americans who have already had their insurance canceled, the low enrollment numbers we have seen so far, and combine that with the website problems, sticker shock, and overall disgust, it is not inconceivable to speculate that by this time next year, **ObamaCare will have caused the number of uninsured in America to increase.**

In today's America, if ObamaCare were a high school sporting contest the "mercy" rule would be invoked to stop the contest. This rule was created to prevent the embarrassment of participants. Regardless of how you feel about the rule itself, apparently there is no embarrassment in Washington. Otherwise this effort to provide a workable health care system would be scrapped and efforts would begin anew.

21 ObamaCare Is A "Weekend at Bernie's" Remake

NOVEMBER 15, 2013

21.1 Weekend at Bernie's

ObamaCare is about to become a remake of *Weekend at Bernie's*.

For those unfamiliar with this film, Wikipedia[1] describes it:

> *Weekend at Bernie's* is a 1989 comedy film[2] directed by Ted Kotcheff[3] and starring Andrew McCarthy[4] and Jonathan Silverman[5] as a couple of young insurance corporation employees who discover their boss is deceased. Believing that they are responsible for his death and that a hit man will not kill them if Bernie is around, they attempt to convince people that he is still alive.

21.2 ObamaCare As Bernie

The movie plot eerily fits the current circumstances of ObamaCare. ObamaCare is Bernie in this re-creation. Like Bernie, **ObamaCare**

---

[1]http://en.wikipedia.org/wiki/Weekend_at_Bernie's
[2]http://en.wikipedia.org/wiki/Comedy_film
[3]http://en.wikipedia.org/wiki/Ted_Kotcheff
[4]http://en.wikipedia.org/wiki/Andrew_McCarthy
[5]http://en.wikipedia.org/wiki/Jonathan_Silverman

is permanently dysfunctional, i.e. dead! Those responsible for ObamaCare must pretend that their version of Bernie is still alive. Their political lives depend on pulling this off so that the hit man (voters) does not take them out.

Government has virtually an unlimited budget to apply to the pretense. They will do and spend whatever is necessary to convince the hit man (voters) that Bernie is still alive and well. But Bernie likely died too soon. The next election is a long way off, especially when trying to prop up a corpse that is beginning to decay.

Time is not an ally in another sense. Wendy McElroy[6] points out that the more that is known about the program the more people will be angered:

> This is the true fatal flaw of Obamacare. The scheme requires those upon whom it depends to abandon their own self-interest in order to further the collective in the name of the Glorious Leader's legacy.

Statists reached for the Gold Ring and got Bernie. They never expected him to arrive at room temperature. Desperate, they now try to convince you he is alive and well. Perhaps they moved too soon and reached too far. It is a long time to the mid-terms. Is it possible disguise a corpse that long, especially one that is decaying and rotting?

This single piece of legislation has the potential to drive a wedge between Obama and the Democrat Party. If it is perceived to be a threat to individual survival (re-election), Democrats may leave ship Obama. This calculation will depend on how they assess their chances of survival. Are they better staying on this ship or jumping overboard and swimming on their own?

---

[6]http://www.thedailybell.com/editorials/34740/Wendy-McElroy-Obamacare-and-the-New-Soviet-Man/

22 ObamaCare: The Dumbest Political Move Ever?

DECEMBER 3, 2013

ObamaCare will likely be viewed by political historians as the dumbest political move ever.

As the program rolls out, the sham becomes increasingly apparent even to the dullards amongst Obama supporters. The Wall Street Journal[1] observed:

> ... the public is learning that ObamaCare's insurance costs more in return for worse coverage.

Mr. Obama and his liberal allies call the old plans "substandard." However, they were not considered substandard by the consumers who selected them. Obama needed this program to implement his version of social equity and income redistribution. Only coincidentally can that match up with some consumer wishes. Certainly it will fail to match up with most.

In their rush to immortality in the Socialist Heroes Hall of Fame, Obama and his fellow Democrats were blinded by the goal. Nationalized health care, the Holy Grail of Socialism, was within their grasp and they went for it. In doing so, they lost sight of the longer-term political implications. This error qualifies ObamaCare as the dumbest political move ever.

---

[1] http://online.wsj.com/news/articles/SB10001424052702303460004579192081764514664

22.1 Health Care Wrecking Ball

Nancy Pelosi famously enhanced her standing in the Legion of Stupids when she uttered her we-must-pass-the-bill-in-order-to-see-what's-in-it nonsense. The bill passed. She (and we) still don't know what is in it. Now, apparently we have to implement it (an arduous task) to learn what is in it.

Each day reveals more of the incompetence and arrogance associated with this monstrosity. Uncertainty and confusion increase as the negatives surface. The incredible lies associated with the bill become apparent as the monstrosity unfolds.

Access to health care and insurance coverage, principal reasons behind the effort, are now being questioned as to their validity. Other than the ideologues who passed the bill, few opinions of the bill have not decreased as more is known about it. Increasing numbers question the costs and the loss of freedom required. Many Democrats and media supporters now see it as potentially career-threatening.

Government incompetence, in terms of its ability to manage anything, has been moved to center stage once again. For Socialists, this issue is one best kept hidden.

The following issues are becoming apparent to the non Kool-Aid set:

- It will destroy the finest health care system in the world.
- It will cause unnecessary suffering and premature deaths.
- It will disrupt lives as insurance coverage is canceled.
- It will raise the costs of insurance.
- It will cause many to lose their doctors.
- It will cause available physician networks to decrease.
- It will produce less health care and less quality.
- It will bend the cost curve unfavorably.

- It will cause rationing ("death panels" if you prefer).

Backers of the plan promised that none of these outcomes would occur.

ObamaCare is likely the dumbest piece of legislation ever. The laws of unintended (and intended) consequences are playing out in ugly fashion. Horrible outcomes for the citizenry and country are assured, but that alone is not enough to gain the title "dumbest political move ever!"

Harming others has never bothered politicians. It is a natural by-product of their work. It takes more than that to qualify as the dumbest political move. Specifically, it takes legislation which harms the legislators who thought it would advance their agenda.

22.2 Political Wrecking Ball

ObamaCare is a dumb political move because it provided **no, zero, zip, nada** political advantage, It provides great political disadvantages for its proponents.

The Democrat Party ramrodded ObamaCare through without a single Republican vote. Few political positions have ever been defined so precisely. Ownership of this political Frankenstein was never in doubt.

Simple mathematics (something that politicians are notoriously not good at) makes the point regarding the political damage associated with the bill. There are 300 million people in the country (actually more, but 300 million is close enough for government work and a nice round number for illustrative purposes). The alleged need for ObamaCare was to cover 30 million of these 300 million who were uninsured. (Some estimates were as high as 45 million, again not meaningful for this purpose.)

The bill was targeted for the 30 million who had no insurance. But Democrats already "owned" 80% or more of these voters. There was no political upside to be gained from this group. The remaining 270 million potential voters were split almost evenly between Democrat and Republican. Vote-seeking among this latter group made sense. Instead this group was foolishly put at risk by Democrats.

The political calculus for buying new voters did make any sense. The potential for gaining votes was in the 270 million. But most of them would be harmed by the legislation.

The Democrat Party knows how to play Santa Claus. It is the basis for their political superiority. It is almost inconceivable that they would seemingly shoot themselves in the foot with this program.

The apparent stupidity does not stop here however. It extends to jeopardizing the Welfare State itself.

22.3 Stupid Socialism

No other welfare program, to my knowledge, has been so clumsily designed as ObamaCare. This program violated the tooth fairy myth of government. That is, they all pretended to provide "freebies." ObamaCare violated this critical principle.

Otto von Bismarck, the generally acknowledged progenitor of the Welfare State, knew there was no tooth fairy but was clever enough to design programs that created this myth. In his words:

> My idea was to bribe the working classes, or shall I say, to win them over to regard the state as a social institution existing for their sake and interested in their welfare.

By spreading costs over a large number of players, Bismarck created the illusion that something was "free." Even if the total cost of a program were known, it was imperative that costs be hidden and small at the payer's level.

The essence of the modern welfare state is a scam dependent on belief in the tooth fairy. Recipients see the "gifts" and assume they are provided by a benevolent and caring State. The actual costs are, to the extent possible, hidden from those actually paying.

ObamaCare violated this critical pillar of the Welfare State. General revenues could not be used given the monetary and fiscal condition of the country. A tax hike was not politically possible and would have jeopardized the "free lunch" myth upon which ObamaCare was sold.

So funding for the program was implemented through the insurance industry in terms of premiums. When people believed their premiums were going to decrease, that was fine. The problem was that premiums had to go up and the costs to each person would be easily identifiable.

Premium payers suddenly saw how they were paying for others and the exact costs that were being incurred. That their insurance protection decreased at the same time only added to their anger.

The ideology must have overwhelmed the proponents of the program. They did not take into account the backlash that would occur. Nor did they seem to recognize what violating the foundational principle of the Welfare State might mean.

The program design must have caused Otto von Bismarck to roll over in his grave. By allowing those with insurance to identify that they were paying for the program violated his century-old rule – "never let the payers know what it cost them" – was violated.

ObamaCare was on its way to killing the tooth fairy myth upon which the socialist state depended. That's probably the most positive comment that can be made about the program.

22.4 Political Insanity

The beneficiaries of the program, to the extent there will be any, were primarily Democrats already. The larger group (270 million) stood to gain nothing unless they fell for Obama's lies.

The larger group already had insurance and 80% were happy with their plans. The majority of the country did not want ObamaCare, even with the lies. Forcing this legislation on the public was akin to poking a hornet's nest with a stick.

People were promised there would be no pain and all gain from ObamaCare. They could keep their old plans and their doctors. They would receive expanded coverage, better insurance and the average family premium would decrease by $2,500 per year. If you were stupid enough to believe this nonsense, what was not to like?

Did Democrats with insurance believe these lies? Many did, after all their leader was still in his Messiah phase and Messiahs don't lie. Nor does government so long as it is run by Democrats.

Now the ObamaCare turkey is home to roost. Most promises were lies. 80 million families are projected to lose their existing insurance coverage. That represents over 200 million of the 270 million group. Whether Republican or Democrat, these people were sold down the river by ideologues blinded by their Holy Grail – nationalized health care.

The lives and budgets of most Americans are in disarray as a result of this legislation. Health care matters will worsen as this program advances. So too will the futile promises and lies coming from Washington. Many Democrat politicians at this point may understand how kamikaze suicide pilots felt.

Republicans and Democrats have been affected. One party is not surprised and is in full "I-told-you-so" mode. The other party is in panic and has a "How-could-they-do this-to-us?" reaction. Many from the latter group will switch sides in the 2014 mid-terms. Few from the first group will.

Tactical Insanity

The political insanity, from a tactical viewpoint, is best understood in light of the following:

1. It couldn't work. Many people knew this before the legislation passed.
2. About 50% of the group that were going to be adversely affected were Democrats.

Strategic Insanity

The funding of ObamaCare unwittingly exposed the myth upon which the Welfare State rests. Democrats are learning that there is no tooth fairy and that their Wunderkind President is just another scheming, lying politician.

From a strategic standpoint this could have enormous effects. The Democrat Party used the tooth fairy for 80 years to dominate US politics.

The Democrat Party likely presented the hapless Republican Party with **the biggest political gift in history**. Democrats shot themselves in the foot (perhaps the head) with the imposition of ObamaCare. The wound threatens the Democrat chances in 2014. However, it may prove to be an existential event for Liberalism and the Welfare State in the long run. Democrats revealed the lie behind the Welfare State.

Liberalism is unlikely to die, but this legislation may mark its zenith. This one single event is apt to mark the turning point for Progressivism. If there is anything positive about ObamaCare, it was this, mostly yet unappreciated, unintended consequence.

23 Joe Isuzu, Our President

NOVEMBER 14, 2013

> *As democracy is perfected, the office of president represents, more and more closely, the inner soul of the people. On some great and glorious day the plain folks of the land will reach their heart's desire at last and the White House will be adorned by a downright moron.* **H. L. Mencken**

What would you get if you crossed Alfred E. Newman with Joe Isuzu? The probable offspring would be something approximating the current President of the United States, at least in terms of approach and abilities.

23.1 Who Was Joe Isuzu?

For the benefit of younger readers, some comments may be in order. Twenty to twenty-five years ago, Isuzu marketed automobiles through a character named Joe Isuzu. Joe made the prototype car salesman look honest. He was an inveterate liar, but a likable one.

The advertisements were deliberately over the top, making Joe and his outrageous claims amusing. Captions below the ad conveyed the obvious – Joe was lying. For those who wish to view one of the old ads, google "Joe Isuzu." I have often thought television sets should provide buttons that can be pushed to flash across the screen: "He's lying." They would be extremely useful watching political debates or listening to the current president.

23.2 President Isuzu

The country elected a version of Joe Isuzu. Unfortunately, our Joe is not funny, likable or harmless. Barack Obama believes he can say (or do) anything he wants. He is not acting and there are real consequences associated with his behavior.

Barack Obama is the Joe Isuzu of politics, without the sub-titles and entertainment value. Joe was fun; Barack is not.

Obama fits the definition of what this non-psychologist understands as a sociopath. He lies routinely and blatantly. He lies even when it is unnecessary. He seems to believe his own lies and shows no shame when caught. He is the national equivalent of Anthony Wiener, without the sex obsession but with his own sociopathic qualities.

Anything good that happens, he takes credit for. Anything bad that happens was George Bush's or someone else's fault. Obama never takes responsibility for his own failures, perhaps because he believes he has never failed.

ObamaCare is the latest example of his pathology. He feigned an apology to those who lost their insurance coverage. Then he admonished them for not listening more carefully to what he had originally said. Unfortunately for him, there are at least thirty instances that show he outright lied and continues to do so.

When something is his responsibility (virtually anything that his Administration does falls into this category), he claims he didn't know about it until he learned it from the media. Then comes his "concern" or "outrage" for the problem followed by his promise to fix it and make sure it never happens again. This phony routine has been repeated several times. There is no evidence that he ever takes any action beyond this show for the media.

Terms like responsibility and accountability are foreign to Obama. Ethics, leadership, management and a host of other terms used to describe accomplished people are rarely used to describe Obama. It is unclear whether he has even heard the terms before.

23.3 Clarence Darrow Was Right

Presidents used to be heroes. Parents used to tell children they could grow up to be president. Now, there is living proof in the White House that almost anyone can become president. Clarence Darrow anticipated Obama:

> When I was a boy I was told that anybody could become President. Now I'm beginning to believe it.

Not anyone can become president, at least not anymore. It takes an unusually abnormal, as in aberrant, person to gain this office. He must be likable and be able to lie without conscience. He must be unusually ruthless because he competes against other sociopaths. Truth and dignity are baggage that must be shed to succeed in this game.

Politicians have become (probably always were) a contemptible lot. Few are normal and very few of these remain that way after their first taste of power. **To achieve the highest rung, you must be the most gifted sociopath.**

Our President Isuzu was an exceptional candidate. He derailed "sure-thing" Hillary and the Clinton machine. He knew how to play hardball, at least on the campaign trail.

Obama is overly arrogant and a loner. He believes himself to be the smartest man in Washington. His messianic delusions add to his problems. He is devoid of shame, even when caught in a blatant lie or misdeed. In short, he is a perfect politician.

His character defects and sociopath tendencies exceeded those of his competitors. He was "the sickest puppy" in the race which undoubtedly assisted his win.

My apologies to Joe Isuzu for using him as a comparison in this piece. He was fun and never hurt anyone. In that regard, he was an inappropriate comparison.

24 Is Obama Done?

NOVEMBER 15, 2013

Is it over for Obama? Has Boy Blunder maneuvered himself into a position from which there is no escape?

The answers to these questions appear to be positive but good politicians have Houdini-like qualities.

Two important conditions suggest that Obama's problems are irreparable.

24.1 1. Humpty Dumpty Broke

ObamaCare was the signature achievement of this Administration. Arguably it is the only achievement and a dubious one at that.

A good metaphor for ObamaCare would be Humpty Dumpty, although Humpty actually functioned until he had his incident with a wall. ObamaCare never functioned and likely never will. It is like Humpty Dumpty who could not be put back together.

The hubris of Socialist planners ensured that something impossibly complex would result from the health care effort. Saboteurs, inserted into the ObamaCare team, could not have done the damage these zealots unintentionally did.

The arrogance of the effort was only exceeded by the hubris of the designers. Central planners think they know everything and that anything can be improved. Friedrich Hayek referred to this attitude as the **"fatal conceit."**

Adam Smith offered his own assessment of such matters (my emboldening):

"The man of system, on the contrary, is apt to be very wise in his own conceit; and is often so enamored with the supposed beauty of his own ideal plan of government, that he cannot suffer the smallest deviation from any part of it. He goes on to establish it completely and in all its parts, without any regard either to the great interests, or to the strong prejudices which may oppose it. He seems to imagine that he can arrange the different members of a great society with as much ease as the hand arranges the different pieces upon a chess-board. He does not consider that the pieces upon the chess-board have no other principle of motion besides that which the hand impresses upon them; but that, in the great chess-board of human society, every single piece has a principle of motion of its own, altogether different from that which the legislature might choose to impress upon it. If those two principles coincide and act in the same direction, the game of human society will go on easily and harmoniously, and is very likely to be happy and successful. **If they are opposite or different, the game will go on miserably, and the society must be at all times in the highest degree of disorder.**"

[H/T Mario Rizzo for this reference from the Liberty Press edition, VI.II.42]

The arrogance of the ObamaCare effort was breathtaking. It represented central planning for 16% of the American economy. There was no leadership to coordinate what became dozens of subgroups working quasi-independently of each other. Even under ideal leadership and coordination, it is doubtful the task could have been accomplished.

Elitists never consider the fact that their way might not be preferred by the people it is imposed upon. These geniuses assume that whatever they think or produce must be superior to that which developed via markets or an evolutionary trial and error process. That is their fatal conceit.

A plan has been put in place that the public wants no part of. It is backed by government coercion and force, but it ignores the wishes of the public. As Adam Smith stated:

> "... the game will go on miserably, and the society must be at all times in the highest degree of disorder."

Government and Socialism enthusiasts were confident in their abilities to achieve the task. Each of the would-be commissars had his own pet ideas of how to improve society. Each included his own versions of controls, "nudges" and coercions. How could anyone believe these pieces would fit together properly? Why would anyone believe they would meet the wants and needs of the public?

Humpty Dumpty was stillborn, but political necessity deemed it be launched anyway. Had it never been launched, the Obama Presidency would not be considered the failure that it is today, although the passage of time likely would have resulted in the same judgment, albeit at a later stage of the presidency.

24.2 2. Personality Not Leadership

Fouad Ajami[1] described this aspect of the problem:

> "Rule by personal charisma has met its proper fate. The spell has been broken, and the magician stands exposed. We need no pollsters to tell us of the loss of

---

[1]http://online.wsj.com/news/articles/SB10001424052702304243904579196440800552408? mod=trending_now_2

faith in Mr. Obama's policies and, more significantly, in the man himself. Charisma is like that. Crowds come together and they project their needs onto an imagined redeemer. The redeemer leaves the crowd to its imagination: For as long as the charismatic moment lasts "a year, an era" the redeemer is above and beyond judgment. He glides through crises, he knits together groups of varied, often clashing, interests. Always there is that magical moment, and its beauty, as a reference point."

Obama's cult of personality still exists, although only among the most devoted (stupid?). **The majority see that he is no god, no manager and no leader.**

Worship has turned to anger. No one likes to be duped. Americans do not appreciate charlatans.

Old magic and bromides cannot solve this problem. They no longer work. Too many people now have caught on and understand the president is a fraud.

24.3 Reason To Worry

As the ObamaCare fiasco becomes more obvious, Democrats who supported this legislation (virtually all of them) will be put at risk. This development provides an interesting sub-plot in advance of the 2014 mid-term elections.

Many Democrat politicians likely knew Obama was a phony from the start. No matter, his popularity and ability to fool the voters was useful. Now that his magic is gone. Obama represents a threat to the political futures of these same Democrats.

The interplay between Democrat politician's self-interest and loyalty to Obama may become very interesting. Survival is the primary concern of all politicians. If Obama diminishes that, any willingness to stand by him will all diminish. Look for this sub-plot to develop and intensify as the 2014 elections approach.

25 Is The President Sane?

NOVEMBER 29, 2013

Questions regarding President Obama's competence have mostly been limited to management abilities, work ethic, honesty and the like. Allison Martinez[1], however, opens an issue that is only whispered about – his mental stability:

> "Claims of grandeur that are not there, claims of accomplishments that have not happened, claims of seeing things that are not real, and claims of false barriers are not the claims of a sane person. President Obama's absurd and contradictory statements are the sort of gibberish that comes from the mouth of mad men. They are *prima facie* evidence that the President is missing some marbles in his cranium and should be removed from office. Mad men have no place in leading a free people and the world's greatest nuclear power.

> The Obama Administration isn't just mismanaging things; Jimmy Carter mismanaged things. No one ever seriously questioned Carter's patriotism or Christianity. They didn't question his sanity, but they did question his competence. Many including myself, have challenged the economic model used by Carter and his belief in Keynesian economics and socialist policies, but no one questioned his character, except perhaps Ted Kennedy and that crowd. While Carter may have missed what was in plain sight to others, he didn't

---

[1]http://freepatriot.org/2013/11/28/wild-claims-president-suggest-may-sane/

make things up. Carter's people didn't lie about the data, although they did often cloak it in terms that were favorable to them. President Obama is beyond anything Jimmy Carter might have done.

This President isn't simply incompetent, he appears not to be sane. He doesn't know the truth from a lie. He makes up stuff, and he sees things that are not there, and he sees himself in a level of grandeur that is not warranted."

This man in the White House is not normal, at least in the sense that most other Presidents have been. Whether clinical psychologists or psychiatrists would agree with Martinez' assessment is unknown. Few have anything to gain, and much to lose, by publicly expressing their opinions.

The strongest evidence for sanity is vice-president Joe Biden. Choosing him as a vice president was a stroke of genius. Joe, you see, is the best job security Obama could have. Biden is a blanket insurance policy against the removal of the president.

This choice of vice president may have been luck or unusually perceptive.

26 Liar-In-Chief

DECEMBER 6, 2013

Let's get serious folks! There is an inveterate liar in the highest office in the land. There is no crime in saying so:

> To announce that there must be no criticism of the president is morally treasonable to the American public.
> **Theodore Roosevelt**

What does a country do when its leader routinely ignores its laws and lies to its citizens? What do people do when policies pave the way to impoverishment, tyranny and eventual enslavement?

Those are the questions confronting the US today. I know it, you know it, many of Obama's supporters know it, Congress knows it, the media knows it, our allies know it and our enemies know it.

Barack Obama is a pathological liar, a disgrace to the office and to the country.

There is no other way to describe this unethical individual. His behavior is disgusting and repulsive to every American who still believes in the Constitution, ethics and integrity. He is the epitome of Dwight D. Eisenhower's cogent observation:

> "Any man who wants to be president is either an egomaniac or crazy."

Obama meets both of Ike's criteria.

Criticism from Obama is beginning to appear frequently. Some spotted it earlier than others and were unrestrained in expressing their opinions. Dr. John[1] said this more than two and a half years ago:

> "It is entirely reasonable to assert that whatever Barack Obama says, it will be false. It is entirely reasonable to assert that one can count on the exact opposite occurring.
>
> You are an idiot if you take him at his word.
>
> Ever."

My thoughts coincided with this position and have for a long time. I thought it inappropriate to be so blunt. Surely things were or would become so obvious that the country would recognize what a mistake it made electing this fraud. It was so obvious that even a fully invested media could not continue to cover for this inept, dishonest charlatan.

Apparently the media has no conscience, integrity or intelligence. They continue to pretend that nothing is wrong and that President Obama is doing a wonderful job.

It is time to drop any pretense regarding this man's competence or integrity. He seems more suited to a psychiatric ward or prison than the highest office in the land. To appreciate some of his lies, read Barack Obama is the biggest liar ever to stain the Presidency of the US[2].

---

[1] http://floppingaces.net/2013/10/27/barack-obama-is-the-biggest-liar-ever-to-stain-the-presidency-of-the-us/

[2] http://floppingaces.net/2013/10/27/barack-obama-is-the-biggest-liar-ever-to-stain-the-presidency-of-the-us/

Citizens are about to enter a period of great adversity as a result of ObamaCare. Many will lose their insurance coverage. Most will end up with higher premiums and less coverage. Health care will deteriorate. The country's economy will take another hit from the disincentives contained in the bill.

This tragedy is just part of a larger plan to impose tyranny on the country. Nothing good can come from this ideological madness. ObamaCare will eventually collapse under its own weight. It is unworkable and unwise. It was from the very beginning. But when it collapses, it may be too late. The nation may then be enslaved to an all-powerful State, the ultimate goal of the program.

That Congress allowed this man to lie so blatantly and to flaunt the Constitution is a dereliction of their Oaths of Office. **They should impeach him and then, themselves, resign in mass.**

Let's push the Reset Button and hope we can rebuild! Whether that is possible at this stage is moot. Regardless, that option will not be available much longer.

27 Peasants With Pitchforks

DECEMBER 16, 2013

Visions of peasants with pitchforks marching on Washington are increasingly popular metaphors for solving the mess in Washington.

Washington will not discipline itself. No political solution can remedy the problems caused by more than a century of political meddling and plunder.

27.1 A New Founding?

Washington loves power and hates constraints. Its progressive deterioration in integrity, morality and respect for the law has reduced it to behavior indistinguishable from that of organized crime. Its practice of tyranny is astounding and rapidly increasing.

If government cannot or will not solve its own problems, what is left? Some believe this point, expressed by Thomas Jefferson in late 1775, has been reached:

> "Believe me, dear Sir: there is not in the British empire a man who more cordially loves a union with Great Britain than I do. But, by the God that made me, I will cease to exist before I yield to a connection on such terms as the British Parliament propose; and in this, I think I speak the sentiments of America."

Times are different. Today people are softer and less principled. They are more easily bought off with "bread and circuses." Government is wealthier and has more bread and circuses with which to divert attention. They also have bigger clubs in the event the bread and circuses fail.

The approach appeared to work in the old Soviet Union where tyranny and repression reigned. However, it took more than seven decades for the tyranny to be overthrown. Perhaps the State merely died of exhaustion.

Where are we? Are we at the beginning of our seven decades or near the end? Have we reached the time "[w]hen in the Course of human events it becomes necessary for one people to dissolve the political bands which have connected them with another and to assume among the powers of the earth, the separate and equal station to which the Laws of Nature and of Nature's God entitle them"?

For those who love liberty and understand its role in this country's rise to greatness, it is easy to reach a conclusion that now is the time to act. But today is not 1775. Different problems and obstacles stand in the way.

27.2 Government and The People

Never before has the US government been so indifferent to the wishes and will of its citizens. A long list of grievances could be cited although the following three demonstrate the point:

- A Rasmussen poll of likely voters says that only 12% favor increased Federal Spending. Yet that is exactly what the new budget agreement ensures.
- Overwhelmingly people want to keep their current health care, yet it is forcibly taken away.
- ObamaCare's defects and failures magnify, yet there is no thought of avoiding the unnecessary pain. Control and power must be served and citizens must (literally) be sacrificed on this altar of the State.

Government is powerful and arrogant. Tyranny is the word that best describes its behavior. The will of the people is ignored. Those who object or speak out are retaliated against, generally by some massive government agency capable of destroying them.

Politicians are concerned only about advancing themselves. Washington has become a colony of parasites, devouring the output of productive citizens and destroying their initiative.

Have we reached the point our forefathers did when they penned the Declaration of Independence? That document was considered treasonous by King George. Does anyone think our current government would react differently to this part of the Declaration of Independence?

> "... whenever any Form of Government becomes destructive of these ends, it is the Right of the People to alter or to abolish it ..."

Is this still a "Right?" The answer to that question is probably obvious and should be troubling.

Two centuries ago the Declaration of Independence was a reflection of the collective content of our character. Today few even know about it. Many guess the quote above is from Karl Marx, Che Guevara or some other crack-pot revolutionary.

We are on the path to ruin, a path traveled so often by other nations. Politicians have no incentive or intent to reverse this course. Few comprehend what is occurring; others just ignore it.

Reversing this course can only be accomplished by reducing State power and control. That has never occurred willingly. Tyranny always expands until people are driven to actions similar to those of our Founders. Will that action be seventy years from now or is it closer?

Understanding where trends lead and altering them are two very different things.

27.3 What Would Happen Today?

History provides clues as to how the State reacts when threatened. Everywhere it strikes back with force and fury. The United States is no exception.

History shows that the US has behaved this way. The Civil War is a prime example and there are others. A smaller and less well known one occurred about eight decades ago. Government history, as taught in government schools, conveniently left this event out of my history and likely yours. Let's review it briefly.

World War I had ended. Government was much less powerful and arrogant then. A new club, the income tax, had recently been enacted but was still small in terms of its effects. The New Deal of Roosevelt had not yet occurred. The Constitution, integrity, equity and honor still mattered. Government was trusted and we still had heroes.

To see the essence of the State, even in those more idyllic times, watch this video[1].

[Interestingly enough this incident concerned our veterans who had returned from the World War I. Based on the recent VA scandal, their treatment hasn't changed.]

The treatment accorded these veterans then surprised me. Do you think any similar attempt would not be dealt with more harshly today? Try to reconcile the role of history's heroes – Douglas MacArthur, Dwight Eisenhower and George Patton – and their roles in this event. They seem to have been on the wrong side. Perhaps that is why most of us know nothing about it.

Given the criminals in charge today, what do you suppose would be the reaction to peasants with pitchforks?

---

[1]http://www.youtube.com/watch_popup?feature=player_embedded&v=sNOsIB5VMSQ

28 Truth Dies First

JANUARY 13, 2014

Integrity and truth are gone in this country, at least with respect to government.

The economy is in shambles yet government insists on telling us that we are in a recovery. Government statistics appear to be routinely manipulated in a fashion to make things look better than they are.

If there is a recovery (there is not!), it is the slowest and longest recovery in history. The recession was declared over in June of 2009. Why are we still recovering? Oh, that we really were recovering!

As government's scam and very existence becomes imperiled by deteriorating conditions, it and its media allies bend whatever truth remains to fit the message they wish to convey. Under such conditions, facts are inconvenient things and dispensed with. We have reached the Orwellian State where words have little meaning and data are routinely manipulated.

It is said that the first casualty of war is the truth. The government is now at war with its people who have lost faith in its leadership. Truth died a while back.

We are close to the stage where government becomes the **cornered, wounded animal that will do anything, anything! to survive.** When matters become existential for government, nothing will be allowed to stand in its way as it fights to survive. More than truth will then be murdered.

Thomas Lifson[1] exposes some of the enormous lies regarding the economic situation in this short piece (Hat tip: Andrew Malcolm):

---

[1] http://www.americanthinker.com/blog/2014/01/m-the_obama_jobs_index.html

The Obama Jobs Index

by Thomas Lifson

The official unemployment rate has become a joke, what with massive numbers of people dropping out of the workforce and therefore becoming invisible. The latest report of a decline in unemployment in the face of a pathetic 74,000 new jobs indicates the uselessness of the figure.

Fortunately, the editors of Investor's Business Daily[2] have come up with their own indices, and they are well worth a look. For example:

6.3 million: Net new jobs created since Obama's recovery started in June 2009

13.8 million: New jobs that would have been created had Obama's kept pace with the average of the previous 10 recoveries.

3.6%: Growth in private jobs since Obama took office.

43%: Growth in the number of temp jobs. (snip)

58.6%: Current employment-to-population ratio.

61%: Ratio when Obama took office.

---

[2]http://news.investors.com/ibd-editorials/011014-686041-counting-the-ways-obama-policies-have-failed-to-create-jobs.htm

62%: Average employment-to-population ratio in the 30 years before Obama took office.

$1,006: Drop in median household income during the 2007-09 recession.

$2,535: Drop in median income after the recession ended in June 2009, according to Sentier Research.

Are any of these statistics suggestive of a recovery? Do any indicate a healthy, growing economy? Despite whatever alterations may have been applied to these numbers, they are dismal and suggestive of an economy in decline rather than recovery.

29 Hopeless Change

JANUARY 17, 2014

Barack Obama's obscure campaign slogan "Hope and Change" has now been defined. For most, it means something closer to "Hopeless Change."

The empty-suit who occupies the presidency has grown old and tiresome. His phony delivery of incessant lies and distortions are worn. So too is his arrogance. In short, he has become a "public nuisance," clogging up roadways, runways and airwaves.

Arrogance is usually a fatal flaw, even when it is accompanied by competence. When it is paired with incompetence, tragedy results. Sadly, this Mountebank-In-Chief has paired extreme arrogance with extreme incompetence, a recipe for extreme disaster.

What must Obama think of the American public? Does he believe they are so stupid as to not see through his shopworn routines? In the age of the internet and ubiquitous cell-phone cameras, even the mainstream media are hard-pressed to cover for him.

He has no cards to play other than those acquired as a community organizer, which itself raises some interesting but embarrassing questions:

- How many in this country ever heard the term "community organizer" before Obama?
- Just what does a community organizer do?
- What are the job qualifications?
- If these skills are useful, why should Al Sharpton or Jesse Jackson not be president? (Both have better resumes than Obama, at least with respect to community organizing.)

- What should a college student choose as a major if he wants a career in community organizing?
- What kind of early job experience prepares one for such a career?

Obama falls back on his community organizing skills, honed while agitating Chicago's poor. Perhaps that is because it is all he has to work with. Perhaps it is because he believes it still works with that portion of his base condemned to ignorance and dependency by his and his Party's policies. Maybe there are now more of them than there are true working people.

He knows little else but class warfare. He has no competence in economics, administration or statesmanship. The University of Chicago Law School should be embarrassed to have put him in a classroom.

What does he think of the increasing number of people turning away from him? What does it say when Bob Gates, hardly a partisan, provides insights about Obama's incompetence in his recent book?

Our economy is in shambles. The International scene is a disaster with enemies emboldened and gaining ground. Allies are becoming former allies, looking for new, trustworthy and dependable partners. The US has lost respect around the world and its commitments are no longer taken seriously.

One of Britain's top Defense advisers suggests Obama is clueless:[1]

> "Sir Hew Strachan, an expert on the history of war, says that the president's strategic failures in Afghanistan and Syria have crippled America's position in the world.

---

[1] http://www.thedailybeast.com/articles/2014/01/15/senior-uk-defense-advisor-obama-is-clueless-about-what-he-wants-to-do-in-the-world.html

> President Obama is "chronically incapable" of military strategy and falls far short of his predecessor George W. Bush, according to one of Britain's most senior military advisors.

> Sir Hew Strachan, an adviser to the Chief of the Defense Staff, told The Daily Beast that the United States and Britain were guilty of total strategic failure in Iraq and Afghanistan, and Obama's attempts to intervene on behalf of the Syrian rebels "has left them in a far worse position than they were before."

The US needs leadership based on competence and integrity. That cannot be provided by the current Administration.

The economic condition of the country, bad when Obama took over, now poses an existential threat to economies everywhere. Much of this results from the failed policies of this Administration.

The geopolitical situation is more threatening. Allies no longer trust us and enemies no longer fear us. Poking at hornet's nests with sticks produced the fury now rampant in the Middle East.

Unlike the economy, there can be little question regarding responsibility for the extremely dangerous and rapidly deteriorating International condition.

Brace yourselves. This will end badly!

30 Hayek, Obama and Serfdom

JANUARY 24, 2014

30.1 The Road To Serfdom

Frederich Hayek's "The Road to Serfdom" describes how societies move from prosperity to poverty and from liberty to authoritarianism.

This instant classic described what Hayek lived through in Germany. He feared that the same policies were being repeated in Great Britain and the United States. The book was written in the 1940s. According to Hayek, these policies would lead to serfdom.

The path was being followed unwittingly, according to the author. He attributed the deterioration to men of good will who didn't understand the perverse outcomes that resulted from what seemed noble policies.

Hayek knew that a weakening in the social and political fabric opened the door for men with bad intentions to assume control. "Why The Worst Get On Top," Chapter Ten in the book, explained the process that led to bad leaders.

Few would argue that Hayek's feared outcome came to pass (yet!). More are concerned about continuing movement down his Road. That is evidenced by the renewed interest in this book. Remarkably, more than half a century after it was written, it reached number one on Amazon. Gene Healy[1], in June of 2010, described its success:

---

[1]http://www.cato.org/blog/hayeks-road-serfdom-1-amazon

"F.A. Hayek's classic *The Road to Serfdom*[2], written 66 years ago, has been in the top 100 on Amazon's bestseller list for the last six days, and hit number 1 today[3]." (h/t Greg Mankiw[4]).

Amazon described the book:

"An unimpeachable classic work in political philosophy, intellectual and cultural history, and economics, *The Road to Serfdom* has inspired and infuriated politicians, scholars, and general readers for half a century. Originally published in 1944; when Eleanor Roosevelt supported the efforts of Stalin, and Albert Einstein subscribed lock, stock, and barrel to the socialist program—"The Road to Serfdom" was seen as heretical for its passionate warning against the dangers of state control over the means of production. For F. A. Hayek, the collectivist idea of empowering government with increasing economic control would lead not to a utopia but to the horrors of Nazi Germany and Fascist Italy."

Hayek's analysis was remarkable. His timing was wrong. Like so many other societal and institutional predictions of decline, the survival abilities were underestimated. Institutions take longer to die than most prognosticators believe.

Nevertheless, the book remains relevant today because we are still on Hayek's road and closer than ever to his feared destination.

---

[2]http://www.amazon.com/Road-Serfdom-F-Hayek/dp/0226320553/ref=sr_1_1?ie=UTF8&s=books&qid=1276106545&sr=1-1

[3]http://www.amazon.com/gp/bestsellers/books

[4]http://gregmankiw.blogspot.com/2010/06/amazon-number-one.html

30.2 Unintended Consequences

Hayek's predictions were based on the plans of well-meaning people who insisted on changes they believed proper. Serfdom was never intended nor thought a possible outcome. Policy proponents were men of good will who aimed to improve society. The Road to Serfdom was a book about "unintended consequences" before the phrase became popular.

Historical Context

Central planning reached its zenith immediately following World War II. Command and control was used to mobilize economies for the war effort. The success in defeating history's greatest horror led many to believe that the "best and brightest" could improve the seemingly chaotic manner in which society developed and operated.

Economic and social processes appeared to develop in a manner that was haphazard. There was no central plan, merely a long evolutionary process based on trial and error. Rational planning could certainly improve outcomes, or so it was thought. That was the intellectual kultursmog post World War II.

Planning

Hayek was not against planning. He argued that planning was necessary and good, but at the individual level not at the level of the State. Individual planning and interaction with markets produced what Hayek termed "spontaneous order." No rational, centralized planning could hope to approximate what was automatically done by free men and free markets. The infinite amount of necessary information made the task impossible.

The Soviet Union adopted the communist model and central planning. Many praised their approach and (lied about) successes. Right up until their collapse, most favoring the Soviet approach believed it to have succeeded spectacularly. Paul Samuelson, considered by many as the leading economist at the time, offered these assessments in his popular economics text:

> "Every economy has its contradictions. What counts is results, and there can be no doubt that the Soviet planning system has been a powerful engine for economic growth." **Paul Samuelson, Economics, 1985 edition**

> "Contrary to what many skeptics had earlier believed, the Soviet economy is proof that a socialist command economy can function and even thrive." **Paul Samuelson, Economics. 1989 edition**

Inconveniently for Mr. Samuelson, the Soviet Union imploded and ceased to exist in 1991.

Hayek was a leading figure in opposing Socialism as a viable economic system. Before the war he continued the work of his mentor, Ludwig von Mises, on the theoretical case for why a Socialist economy would fail. Hayek lived to see this prediction come true, at least with respect to the USSR.

Today theoretical economic arguments have been substantiated by historical outcomes. Socialism and the centrally-controlled economies are now believed to be inefficient and unsustainable.

Theory and empirics dissuade all but extreme ideologues. Government is increasingly questioned as the vehicle to make things better. At least that is the trend outside of capitols like Washington, DC and the so-called intellectual centers of academe.

30.3 Intended Consequences

Barack Obama entered office with the stated goal of transforming America. It is now apparent what he meant! President Obama, quite simply, wants to implement full-blown Socialism in the United States. "Social justice" (an indefinable term) motivates the man and political power is his means. Common sense and history are ignored in his pursuit.

Regardless of how you feel about Socialism, the world is different from that which Hayek confronted in his "Road To Serfdom." Hayek dealt with the issue of unwittingly transforming society into something never intended or desired.

Today the current President of the United States aims directly at what Hayek feared. **Hayek's unintended consequences are now Obama's intended consequences.**

Socialism has been discredited in the eyes of all but the most stubborn ideologues. The Welfare States of Europe have struggled for decades with the pernicious effects of Socialism. Economic growth is anemic. Governments are insolvent. Governments strain under the promises and obligations which are impossible to honor.

Eastern Europeans experienced life under Socialism and are among its strongest opponents. Only pseudo-intellectuals and power-seeking politicians support Socialism.

No man in America's highest office ever openly advocated for Socialism until this current president. His effort comes at a time when Socialism is discredited and on the wane. Both theory and history are inconsistent with his position. Blind ideology is his guide.

31 The State Of The Union Speech

JANUARY 28, 2014

The State of the Union will be reported on by the President of the United States this evening. There is no purpose in watching this phony-baloney dog and pony show. Sadly, the state of our Union is disgraceful.

Nothing is going to change; nor is the true state of the country going to be discussed. If it were, politicians would have to run for their lives.

Simon Black put together what he believes an appropriate State of the Union speech should contain. If you are foolish enough to listen this evening, you will not hear any of this. But it all needs to be said!

Mr. Black's version of the speech[1] that needed to be given:

> "Mr. Speaker, Mr. Vice President, members of Congress, fellow citizens:
>
> This summer we will commemorate the 100th anniversary of the start of World War I.
>
> This senseless, destructive war was started and championed by politicians who cared nothing for the 9 million people who lost their lives.

---

[1]http://www.sovereignman.com/trends/the-real-state-of-the-union-in-just-889-words-13430/

And in doing so, they began a century of warfare which continues to this day.

Our military industrial complex is larger than ever. We have nearly 2 million troops and national guardsmen, plus 3.5 million civilians employed in the defense sector.

With such awesome capabilities, we continue to resort to violence and death to exact political goals which benefit a tiny elite.

All of this has created a police state in the Land of the Free that is a far cry from the country we all grew up in.

Your government has spawned a culture of fear and intimidation. Nearly every federal agency, including the Fish and Wildlife Service, has its own gun-toting police force to pistol-whip citizens into submission.

And we're stocking up. Your government has recently procured 1.6 BILLION rounds of hollow-point ammunition to supplement our existing supplies.

But frankly, we don't need guns to harass citizens.

Our tax authorities have become more threatening than mafia warlords. The plunder is so severe that record numbers of Americans are renouncing their citizenship and leaving the country.

There are now dozens of federal, state, and local agencies and courts which have the power to confiscate your assets without any due process.

In addition to your house, your business, and your savings, we also have the authority to take your children away from you as if they are property of the state.

We are here to tell you what you can and cannot put in your own body, or whether you can collect rainwater that falls on own property.

In fact, on any given business day, the federal government issues hundreds of pages of new 'rules', proposed regulations, draft bills, executive orders, and/or regulatory notices.

And if you are not compliant with these rules, you may be committing a crime. Whether you know it or not.

When this nation was founded, there were four federal crimes on the books. Today there are THOUSANDS. Plus we have millions of government employees at all levels to enforce the penalties.

All of this, of course, is financed by you the tax slave.

You (plus unborn generations) are the poor suckers charged with paying off the national debt we politicians have created.

Officially the debt is just north of $17 trillion. But if you include Social Security and pension shortfalls, the figure is several times higher.

You'll never know for sure because we have become masters of deceit regarding official statistics, whether inflation, unemployment, or our liabilities.

But the situation is so dire that the Congressional Budget Office projects the Social Security Administration's disability insurance trust fund to RUN OUT by 2017.

We get by year after year by increasing the debt. And at well over 100% of GDP, we have truly reached the point of no return.

We are now in a position where we must default. Either we must default on our national debt, or we must default on our obligations to you the citizens.

We may end up stealing your savings. Robbing your Social Security. Taxing you to death. Or simply inflating away the value of our debt.

Naturally, we're going to screw you in the process somehow, so be prepared for that. Especially the inflationary tidal wave that's coming.

Our central bank has expanded its balance sheet at an unprecedented pace, creating massive asset bubbles in its wake. These asset bubbles have disproportionately benefited the ultra-wealthy at the expense of everyone else.

Such wanton money printing has also been tremendously destructive to our credibility. Other nations worry about our reckless irresponsibility. That's why we keep spying on them.

Make no mistake: the consequences of our actions are here. And the days of the United States as the world's dominant superpower are finished.

As the decline hastens, we will struggle to sell our debt to the world and to ship our dollars abroad. Fewer nations will be interested in our empty promises.

And without the generosity of other nations loaning us money at record low interest rates that fail to keep pace with inflation, you will really be screwed.

When this happens, you can absolutely count on us to clamp down even harder on the economy and control even more of your lives. For your own good, of course.

No, this may not be the country that you all grew up in. But it is the state of our union, whatever remains of it.

And so my fellow Americans, I urge you to grab your ankles and get ready for a little 'shared sacrifice'.

But don't worry about me, or my senior staff. We will leave government with cushy pensions, $750,000 speaking fees, board seats on public companies, and top positions in the industries that we have accommodated at your expense.

And of course I will be paid handsomely for the arrogant memoirs I will write in which I deny any responsibility for the shit I've gotten you all into.

So when I say "shared sacrifice", I really mean "your sacrifice".

Thank you. God bless you, and God bless these United States of America."

Short, to the point and no nonsense about inequality, obstruction, pens or phones. So clear that even Obama supporters might understand.

32 The Diminished State of The New York Times

JANUARY 29, 2014

It is sad for those of us who remember America in earlier and better times. Institutions, ideals, and hopes continue to crumble as America slides toward mediocrity and worse. This late-starting country rose like a rocket from a backwoods frontier to the envy of the world. Now it has run out of fuel and is in descent.

The reason for the meteoric rise to greatness and prosperity can be explained in one word – freedom. People free to pursue their own interests as they defined them produced the greatest economic miracle the world has ever seen. This pursuit of self-interest produced the most compassionate people in the world and the means to express that compassion.

The spirit, energy and initiative rose up from the bottom. It has now been crushed by a command and control mentality from the top. The Founders provided a framework that protected people from strong and oppressive government. It was effective for about two centuries. Now that remarkable document, the Constitution, is considered a roadblock to progress.

The US has become just another State characterized by corrupt government. The Constitutional boundaries that contained the evil were overrun. The resulting predatory State now destroys the spirit and initiative of what once was the freest and most prosperous country in the world.

One of the great newspapers of the world used to be The New York Times. Now it is the propaganda arm of the Progressive movement.

Its definition of "all the news fit to print" has a different meaning today than it did fifty years ago.

The following editorial[1] regarding President Obama's State of the Union speech is the latest example of the nonsense and partisanship that passes for news today. My commentary is interspersed.

The Diminished State of the Union[2]

By THE EDITORIAL BOARD January 28, 2014

> Every winter since 2009, President Obama has stood at the podium of the House and pleaded for the co-operation of Congress. For the last three State of the Union speeches, he has largely been ignored. That has left a growing trail of unfinished business: background checks for gun buyers, immigration reform, a higher minimum wage, tax fairness, universal preschool."

For the first couple of years, the Democrats controlled both houses of Congress and Obama got virtually whatever he wanted.

What he wanted and what Congress delivered so scared the American public that they rebelled and gave Republicans control of the House in 2010. That was not done in order to advance Obama's agenda but to stop or derail it. Although the elitists at the NY Times may not understand, many oppose the litany of "unfinished business" they list above.

> "This year was different. Mr. Obama's speech on Tuesday night acknowledged the obvious: Congress has become a dead end for most of the big, muscular uses of government to redress income inequality and improve

---

[1] http://mobile.nytimes.com/2014/01/29/opinion/the-diminished-state-of-the-union.html

[2] http://mobile.nytimes.com/2014/01/29/opinion/the-diminished-state-of-the-union.html

the economy for all, because of implacable Republican opposition. As a result, the remainder of Mr. Obama's presidency will be largely devoted to a series of smaller actions that the White House can perform on its own.

"America does not stand still, and neither will I," he said. "So wherever and whenever I can take steps without legislation to expand opportunity for more American families, that's what I'm going to do."

Taking the offensive by veering around Congress *isn't new*[3] for the administration, but it is more important than ever. As the president forcefully described, inequality has deepened and upward mobility has stalled. If Republicans in Congress stymie the public's needs and desires, Mr. Obama should employ every tool in his box to bypass those barriers. The multistate tour that he plans in the coming days will give him a chance to be even more critical of Congress than he was in the House chamber."

Our system was designed with the intent that Congress be allowed to be a "dead end." That was a deliberate feature in the Founder's thinking. Three **equal** branches of government were created in order to protect against one overstepping its bounds.

Blinded by ideology the NY Times selectively cheers or jeers this behavior depending on who is in office and what is being proposed. When the system inhibited George Bush from pursuing goals they disapproved of, there were no complaints. Now these same safeguards which protect us get criticized because they stand in the way of the Utopian fantasies at the NY Times.

---

[3]http://www.nytimes.com/2012/04/23/us/politics/shift-on-executive-powers-let-obama-bypass-congress.html

Should basic principles no longer guide institutions like government or the media? Do the ends justify the means so long as they coincide with the wisdom emanating from The Grey Lady?

> "Most of the executive actions in the speech have the potential to make a difference, though their diminished scope demonstrates the lost potential caused by political intransigence. Raising the minimum wage to $10.10 an hour for federal contract workers[4] might benefit only a few hundred-thousand people, but it increases the pressure on other businesses and, ultimately, Congress to raise the wage for everyone. (The $10.10 wage, however, provides an income too paltry to celebrate as a huge achievement.)
>
> The increased focus on federal job-training efforts and manufacturing institutes could help reduce unemployment by improving job skills to match the market, as will a $100 million competition to goad high schools into improving science, technology and math learning[5]. A new retirement account could help people save money.
>
> But he left out an executive ban on discrimination by contractors against employees based on sexual orientation and gender identity. That would have made a strong statement about fairness in spending taxpayer money. He could also have prohibited contractors from retaliating against employees who disclose or seek salary information, which would help women know when they are being paid less."

---

[4]http://takingnote.blogs.nytimes.com/2013/09/26/federal-contractors-low-wages/
[5]http://www.nytimes.com/numberscrunch

The economic ignorance in these three paragraphs is staggering. Raising the price of anything reduces the demand. That is the most basic rule of economics and observed behavior. Minimum wage legislation is not an exception.

The second paragraph is especially pitiful. Fix the schools, don't continue to subsidize them. Let's have competition in education so that the poor have access to decent schools. How does a new retirement account help people save money who have none and are unemployed to boot?

Employers discriminating against and victimizing some in society is always good filler for liberal newspapers. The inconsistency of this canard with other canards of the Left doesn't matter to ideologues. On one hand it is claimed that business' self-interest and pursuit of profit dominates all its decisions. On the other hand it is claimed that businesses discriminate against some workers. These hypotheses cannot both be true. If a business wants to maximize profits and some resource or input is under-priced relative to its productivity, that resource will be hired. Otherwise they are not maximizing profits.

Such inconsistencies in stereotyping do not bother ideologues so long as the claim fits the meme they want to convey. Inconsistencies in their thinking is OK, apparently because "they care" so much that they are immune from either criticism or the laws of logic.

> "The only way to truly affect the economy on a mass scale, and to make a difference for tens of millions of people instead of a few hundred thousand, is to persuade Congress to go along on the major initiatives the president was forced to repeat in his remarks, such as extending jobless benefits, creating high-quality preschool for all 4-year-olds, and especially raising the minimum wage.
>
> "This will help families," he said of the wage. "It will

> give businesses customers with more money to spend.
> It doesn't involve any new bureaucratic program. So
> join the rest of the country. Say yes. Give America a
> raise."

This editorial becomes more embarrassing with each paragraph. How about "the only way to truly affect the economy on a mass scale" is to **get the hell out of its way**. Keep government's hands off and the economy will recover just fine, thank you.

Despite how much the Left favors pre-school education, all studies show that the effects are inconsequential after a short period of time. If you are an ideologue spending other people's money that doesn't seem to matter.

> "One particularly promising request the president made
> of Congress was to expand the earned-income tax
> credit, which now benefits 15 million families a year, *to
> workers without children*[6]. That would not only boost
> the incomes of many at the bottom of the ladder,
> but it would provide the incentive to work that many
> Republicans say they support."

What? I fail to see how this provides an incentive to work unless you believe that **taxes are a disincentive to work**. Is the NY Times willing to admit that? Their proposal might be considered more sincere if it also addressed many of the hundreds of other welfare subsidies that truly do penalize work. Memory may fail me, but I don't recall the NYT ever advocating the discontinuance of any government program, dysfunctional or not.

> "Pushing for a vote would reveal whether Republicans
> are so opposed to anything Mr. Obama wants that

---

[6]http://www.nytimes.com/2013/10/13/opinion/sunday/its-not-only-mothers-and-children.html

they would reject their own ideas. As important as executive orders can be, they should not replace showing that Republicans are voting against the public's wishes."

Amazing! The NY Times is not concerned about the Constitutionality of executive orders. Exposing Republicans as an evil is more important for them than any concern about the Constitution.

Politicians in both parties are unpopular. According to the polls, this unpopularity is a bigger problem for Democrats than Republicans. What the public wishes, at least on a grand scale, is to reduce Washington's roles in their lives. Apparently, they believe obstructionism (if that is what the NY Times wants to call it) is better than the alternative. The mid-term elections seem to be polling that way.

The old Grey Lady is getting long in the tooth and increasingly senile. Her time grows short and her bark no longer is feared. Another once-great institution is going by the way-side, partly as a result of the nonsense expressed above.

For a different reaction to the State of The Union speech, look at this Cato Institute video[7].

[7]http://www.economicnoise.com/2014/01/29/diminished-state-union-new-york-times/

33 Mafia Government?

FEBRUARY 7, 2014

Bill Tatro wrote an article entitled "Obama – A Well-known Weakling On The World Stage[1]." It is worth reading.

His description of the perplexing aspects of Republican behavior was particularly relevant:

> "What's most intriguing is not the skill level of the world leaders in exploiting Obama's weakness for their own advantage, but the total ineptness of the Republican leadership in doing the same thing. From Boehner to McConnell, from House to Senate, and from conservative to RINO, they all seem to fail when it comes to making the most out of Obama's day-to-day blunders. It would appear that since these Republican leaders are all cut from the same political cloth regardless of labels, they all have the same goals, namely reelection, and thus cannot do the right thing for the benefit of our country. Needless to say, it gets a little frustrating watching our so-called political opposition leadership continue to miss opportunity after opportunity of exposing the lies, corruption, and incompetence of our current president. Perhaps it's because the so-called political opposition suffers with the same problems in exposing the "emperor's new clothes," which would only expose their own."

---

[1]http://finance.townhall.com/columnists/billtatro/2014/02/06/obama--a-wellknown-weakling-on-the-world-stage-n1790401?utm_source=thdailypm&utm_medium=email&utm_campaign=nl_pm

He hit the nail on the head with the last sentence. It is an explanation that might explain Republican inability or unwillingness to provide effective opposition.

Few in Washington are clean. They are in a profession that encourages illegality. Most political figures have skeletons in their closets that they would prefer remain there, with the door kept closed. Affairs, unethical/illegal business dealings, political kickbacks, indiscretions etc. likely exist for virtually everyone. These are men of power and privilege. To get ahead they cannot have the same ethical calculus as a normal citizen. **They don't become millionaires on what they are paid above the table.**

Given the obvious lack of integrity and Chicago thuggery of the current Administration, how many of these skeletons are still secret? No, they are not available to the general public, but how many are not known by the NSA?

The real threat of the NSA is less from collecting information on citizens than it is collecting information on opponents. Congressmen, high-ranking judges, military officers, political allies etc. can all be blackmailed if improprieties can be discovered.

J. Edgar Hoover developed and perfected the blackmail model. He collected information improperly and illegally on anyone who could possibly challenge him. He did so when it was much harder to do. No one dared cross him, understanding the consequences would be the equivalent of political suicide. Hoover acquired the ability to blackmail most in power. As a result, he retained his position forever and was rarely challenged.

What do you suppose Hoover could have done with NSA technology? Suppose you were a Chicago thug and had this agency and its resources at your command. Would you not take advantage? We know that political hardball is played this way in Chicago. We know that money and other grants are fed to political supporters and allies. Why shouldn't the IRS go easy on friends and tough on enemies? Why would a valuable tool like the NSA, not be used for political advantage?

Once this asset is recognized and exploited, what is not possible? Was the General Petraeus resignation forced under such circumstances? What about John Roberts? The Chief Justice of the Supreme Court inexplicably provided the critical vote that enabled ObamaCare to survive. Is there a more plausible hypothesis about his strange vote? Does blackmail explain what appears to be hapless Republican opposition?

I am not a conspiracy theorist. However, coercion and threats are an important modus operandi for government. Government is force. It is not a game of croquet. The ends today are considered too important to play by the rules if they can be obtained faster and easier via other means. Unethical and illegal are mere words. The ends are what are important. Why not use the IRS against political opponents? Why not lie to the country in order to get re-elected? Why not select cabinet heads who will use whatever means to meet the ends? Why not have a Department of Justice which sees justice not impartially but through a political lens?

All of these musings are speculative. However, human nature is pretty predictable. Power is always abused.

If this speculation is close to the mark, then this country is lost. There is no way that the NSA will not be used against political enemies just as the IRS has been. And it doesn't matter who is in power. Power always corrupts. Whatever might be happening today will grow only worse in the future.

Government will become indistinguishable from the Mafia. It is already more dangerous in that there is no countervailing force to constrain it.

Not even the opposing party which craves power as much as the ruling party will be able to stand up against these practices. They must go along in order to get along. They must protect their own personal roles in this Mafia. Eventually they hope to ascend to the top rung where they get to abuse the power.

There is nothing to stop this devolution from continuing.

34 The IRS Scandal

FEBRUARY 9, 2014

Government lies. Often! As matters become more dangerous for government, the lies increase in frequency and size.

The IRS non-scandal scandal is real! So too are many of the other "non-scandals." Government as practiced by the current administration, considers itself immune to law, ethics or morality. It is a government bent on the acquisition of power regardless of the means used.

Listen to Cleta Mitchell[1] detail her experience with the IRS. This is scary stuff, especially so when the President is willing to blatantly lie about what is going on and has a Justice Department willing to run interference for him.

I am not sure how many times that Ms. Mitchell uses the term "lies" in her testimony, only that it is a lot and likely not enough.

Government has become a predatory monster, running over anyone in its way in its goal to gain complete and total control of over everything and everybody.

---

[1]http://www.economicnoise.com/2014/02/09/government-lies-irs-scandal/

35 President Albatross – An American Tragedy

FEBRUARY 12, 2014

Barack Obama is an albatross. No, not literally a bird. Merriam Webster[1] defines albatross as follows:

> a : something that causes persistent deep concern or anxiety
> b : something that greatly hinders accomplishment

Politically-speaking, Obama is an albatross. He is radioactive, a serious liability for many Democrats trying to extend their careers.

By any objective measure Obama has failed:

- The economy is in shambles. Incomes are shrinking. Welfare rolls are expanding. Unemployment is historically high (when measured properly).
- Confidence in the future is abysmally low.
- Confidence in the Washington political class is at an all-time low.
- Foreign policy is a disgrace, leading to an increasingly and unnecessarily dangerous world.
- Government is insolvent and being made more so by profligate spending. Defaults are inevitable.

---

[1]http://www.merriam-webster.com/dictionary/albatross

- Obama's signature program, ObamaCare, is a Rube Goldberg contraption (apologies to Rube) that is unwanted, unneeded, unimplementable and unworkable. The hubris of the Obama Administration and the Democrat Party demands they protect this stillborn program. To them it represents the Holy Grail. Fewer choices, lower quality providers, higher premiums, higher deductibles and unnecessary fear and consternation to millions of Americans are of little concern if it can be advanced.

President Obama has made life unnecessarily harder for most citizens not in the so-called 1%. That is especially so for his supporters who tend to be poorer and suffer the most from the lack of jobs and opportunity.

Obama has moved the country closer to full-blown Socialism. If that is his goal, then he has been successful. What appeared to be bizarre behavior seems less so when viewed in that light.

In virtually every conventional aspect of government, however, he has failed miserably and embarrassed his supporters. Even the media who sponsored him is beginning to question his abilities publicly.

Obama's "achievements" doom more people to poverty, restrict freedom and create more slaves dependent on government. He has moved the country in the wrong direction and done so more than his opponents assumed possible.

35.1 Obama's World

What is it that makes this man tick? He seems unable or unwilling to recognize reality. Like a peacock, he struts around believing that he is a great and successful leader, "the one we are waiting for." His is a world lacking duty, honor, responsibility, reality or accountability.

His is also a life devoid of any accomplishment other than fooling many of the people at election time.

Obama lives in a fantasy land. There is little room for friends or reality in his space. His aloofness seems to protect him from the laughter and disgust that increasingly displaces the early adulation.

Obama is a charlatan, little more than a common street hustler in a fine suit. The artificial universe inside the Beltway considers him real. Republicans are wary of confronting him, even when he violates the law. Is it possible that Chicago-style retribution explains the lack of resistance? Respect is absent, but apparently not fear.

Like Kim Jong Un, North Korea's nut job, Obama needs to be worshiped. Both are tyrants who believe they are entitled to impose their will as they pretend to serve the people. Obama simply has more constraints. In both instances lives are being diminished and possibilities foregone, yet each leader expects gratitude for whatever scraps are made available.

35.2 History Will Judge

Historians will have a field day analyzing the Obama phenomenon. Here are but a handful of the issues:

- What made the public think this man could run a hot dog stand never mind a country?
- What were the psychological disorders that drove him?
- Why was so obvious an empty suit elected to a second term?
- Why did Congress routinely allow him to run roughshod over the Constitution?

These are puzzling questions, likely to become more important when the full damage to the economy, country and world is recognized. Obama will not be judged favorably in the course of time. The American people who elected this political version of Elmer Gantry are ultimately to blame. Surely their mass psychosis will fascinate future historians and social psychologists.

35.3 The Political Implications

Obama is a true ideologue, one who pursues his goals ruthlessly. He is effective from afar, not up close. Unlike Bill Clinton, he doesn't work to make people like him; he just assumes they do. He has always been a loner, even before politics. Whether he is antisocial or doesn't want people to get close to him for fear they discover his true self is moot. It is likely a bit of both.

His obscurity was instrumental in his rise to power, probably the key to his winning the first time. An unknown man, speaking in platitudes, was treated like a blank slate. People could and did define him in terms of what they wanted. As a blank slate, Obama could become all things to many people.

When President Obama was riding high he was the toast of the town. He was the Democrat meal ticket. Whether he was or could be liked was irrelevant. **He could be used.** Democrats "liked" him when he was useful in terms of their careers, popularity, re-elections and furthering Party goals. To most politicians that is the bottom line, all that matters.

That was then, but it is no more. Obama is no longer a stranger. People now know him. He is far from the Messianic image he cultivated.

There will be no coattails for Democrats in the upcoming elections. John Fund[2] describes the problem:

> "Kevin Faulconer recaptured the mayor's office in San Diego for Republicans in a special election yesterday.

---

[2] http://www.nationalreview.com/corner/370910/obama-turnout-machine-crashes-san-diego-loses-mayors-race-nine-points-john-fund

The polls were skin-tight leading into yesterday's election, and unions poured in millions to keep control in the nation's eighth-largest city.

But in the end the vaunted Obama election model, flood the zone with negative attack ads and excite the base of the Democratic party, flopped. Faulconer defeated fellow City Council member David Alvarez by nine points in a city that Barack Obama carried by 63 percent to 37 percent only 15 months ago."

Obama no longer has any pull for other Democrats. He is now a political albatross, a liability. The love relationship between Obama and the Democrats ended when he became an albatross.

35.4 An American Tragedy

Democrats willingly accepted this charlatan because he could advance their agenda. Now he has become a threat to their livelihood.

Obama's place in history may well be viewed as a tragedy, both for the country and him personally. He came with the greatest accolades and expectations. He will leave without any fanfare and America will likely undo most of his efforts.

Obama's greatest accomplishment is likely to be the fact that he got elected – twice! He will go down in political history as the Elmer Gantry of politics. His greatest failure is that he delivered nothing, despite the elevated expectations and hope that entered office with him.

The ultimate tragedy is likely to occur in the latter stages of his presidency. Democrats up for election or re-election are already treating him as if he had a contagious disease. They do not want to be associated with him or his signature piece of legislation,

ObamaCare. He increasingly finds it difficult to have elected representatives appear with him when he comes to their districts.

If the 2014 elections prove to be a rout of Democrats, then Obama may have an uncomfortable remaining period in office. His ability to pass any new legislation of note is already over. He accomplished nothing other than the passage of the ill-fated ObamaCare. That legislation was instrumental in turning the public against him and the Democrat Party.

If the 2014 elections are a rout as some pundits are predicting, Democrats will blame Obama and his policies. They and Republicans will strip him of what little power he has left, including his legally questionable, and highly ineffective, "pen and phone."

35.5 Ethics in Washington

If there were any honor or integrity in Washington the Democrats would converge on Obama's office like the Republicans did with Richard Nixon. A massive defeat in the 2014 elections might drive them to at least this level of pretend integrity.

Obama may do to the Democrats what Republicans could not. He might return his Party to minority status.

When usefulness is your only chip and that disappears, the lack of real friends can be dangerous. In politics or life, when your usefulness is over, you need friends. Obama has none. This may prove to be pivotal in the last two years of his Administration.

When the Washington Post, a bastion of liberalism, publishes articles like the following[3], one has to wonder just how much support is left for the once Wunderkind:

Obama's ambassador nominees are a disservice to diplomacy

[3]http://www.washingtonpost.com/opinions/obamas-ambassador-nominees-are-a-disservice-to-diplomacy/2014/02/06/2273ef9e-8e86-11e3-b227-12a45d109e03_story.html

By Henri J. Barkey, Published: February 6

Henri J. Barkey is a professor of international relations at Lehigh University. He served on the State Department's policy planning staff from 1998 to 2000.

Two Norwegian lawmakers have nominated Edward Snowden[4], the bete noire of U.S. intelligence, for the Nobel Peace Prize. It is quite possible that this is the Norwegians' way of showing their displeasure and shame at having the Obama administration nominate a completely unqualified person to be its ambassador to Oslo.

The nominee, a Long Island campaign bundler named George Tsunis[5], made a fool of himself during his Senate confirmation hearings[6] last month. He was unaware of some of the most basic facts about Norway. He admitted never having set foot in the country, and he seemed to think that Norway, a monarchy, has a president. He also had no idea which political parties constituted Norway's governing coalition, even though, as ambassador, he would be dealing with them. It seemed, as some later tweeted, that Tsunis had not even bothered to read the Wikipedia page for Norway.

President Obama does a disservice to Norwegians, to himself and, above all, to the people of the United

---

[4]http://www.washingtonpost.com/blogs/the-switch/wp/2014/01/29/edward-snowden-has-been-nominated-for-a-nobel-peace-prize/

[5]http://www.allgov.com/news/appointments-and-resignations/ambassador-to-norway-who-is-george-tsunis-131207?news=851850

[6]http://www.washingtonpost.com/politics/obama-ambassador-nominees--baucus-bell-and-tsunis--hit-bumps-in-hearings/2014/01/30/824d6b40-89e8-11e3-a5bd-844629433ba3_story.html

States by sending such an unqualified person to represent him and us in the capital of a long-standing NATO ally. (I wonder if Tsunis knows that Norway is a member of NATO and not the European Union.) Instead of goodwill, he is engendering anti-American sentiment. Norwegians are likely to conclude that all they are worth to Obama is about $1.3 million[7] – the sum Tsunis bundled or contributed to Obama's reelection campaign and other Democratic efforts in 2012.

The United States claims to value the efforts of diplomats – a point the president reiterated in his State of the Union speech[8] last week. So why do so many seem to think that diplomacy is a profession that anyone can engage in? If you had a plumbing problem, would you call your friendly ambassador to fix it? What message is the president sending to Foreign Service officers and to former and current ambassadors of distinction?

The Obama administration's appointments suggest that the president isn't being honest when he says that diplomacy is important to him. Yet the administration clearly values diplomacy – officials, including the president, have emphasized that the ongoing negotiations with Iran are the way to resolve the nuclear impasse. Would Obama consider making Tsunis our negotiator? Of course not. Yet it's illogical, and insulting, to presume that Norwegians are such wonderful and civilized people – and hence unlikely to cause any problems with Washington – that we can afford to

---

[7] http://news.yahoo.com/watch-what-happens-when-obama-picks-a-top-donor-as-ambassador-161931672.html

[8] http://www.washingtonpost.com/politics/full-text-of-obamas-2014-state-of-the-union-address/2014/01/28/e0c93358-887f-11e3-a5bd-844629433ba3_story.html

send someone on a taxpayer-funded three-year junket to enjoy the fjords.

Even the argument that Norway is an unproblematic post for a political appointee does not pass muster. Obama's ambassador-designate to Hungary, Colleen Bradley Bell[9], is a television soap opera producer ("The Bold and the Beautiful") and also was a money-handler[10] for the president's reelection campaign. What qualifications does she have to be ambassador to a country in crisis? Hungary's democratic institutions are under severe threat from the governing party, and extremists have been targeting minorities. Hungary is a member of both NATO and the European Union. Unfortunately, when asked by Sen. John McCain, Bell was incapable of identifying the U.S. strategic interests in Hungary[11].

This is not a criticism of political appointees per se. There are times when a political appointee is far more suitable for an appointment than a career ambassador. The Saudis have always taken comfort from having someone close to the president appointed ambassador, in the belief that such a person would provide better access to the White House. I have my doubts, but they may be right.

There have also been political-appointee ambassadors who would have rivaled, and possibly surpassed, the best the State Department could produce. One such

---

[9]http://hungary.usembassy.gov/pr_11062013.html

[10]http://www.opensecrets.org/pres12/bundlers.php

[11]http://www.washingtonpost.com/politics/obama-ambassador-nominees--baucus-bell-and-tsunis--hit-bumps-in-hearings/2014/01/30/824d6b40-89e8-11e3-a5bd-844629433ba3_story.html

person is Felix Rohatyn[12], an investment banker who managed New York's financial crisis negotiations in the 1970s. President Bill Clinton appointed Rohatyn, a fluent French speaker, ambassador to France. He was extraordinary; I served in the State Department then, and at times colleagues and I would read Rohatyn's diplomatic cables – he wrote many himself – for the sheer pleasure of their clarity, analysis and style. He probably knew as many people in Paris as he did in New York. As an American, you could not be anything but proud to have Rohatyn as ambassador. Unfortunately, some current nominees are a modern version of the 18th-century French practice of the sale of offices. Then, the income derived went to finance state activities; now, it is for financing campaigns.

Both Democrats and Republicans reward those who helped their campaigns. But for a president who just told the nation of his commitment to reducing in-equality, this practice of rewarding unqualified people, whose "good deed" is to have bundled campaign funds, is particularly jarring."

Pretty tough stuff coming from a liberal newspaper.

---

[12]https://csis.org/expert/felix-g-rohatyn

36 Failure and Criticism

MARCH 2, 2014

Chicago gangsters are tough, but not as tough as Russian gangsters. Pretty-boy Obama is finding that out when dealing with Putin.

Nothing Obama has touched has gone well. Domestically the economy is in shambles. Five years after a recession was declared over, there are still few signs of recovery.

Much of the stagnation is due to Obama's policies, especially that Rube Goldberg contraption that we refer to as ObamaCare. **It does not work, will not work and cannot work!** But our man-child president has never made a mistake in his life, so don't look for him to try and fix it. Any future efforts on his part will be limited to preventing its repeal or protecting Democrats from its harm.

Internationally, the implications of Obama's weakness are metastasizing. The disdain in which Obama is held by other leaders around the world is palpable. He has emboldened enemies and driven allies away. Even the Washington Post, an uber-liberal newspaper, which has consistently defended Obama, appears to have soured. Here is a lead-in to an article WaPo published recently[1]:

> "For much of his time in office, President Obama has been accused by a mix of conservative hawks and liberal interventionists of overseeing a dangerous retreat from the world at a time when American influence is needed most.

[1] http://www.washingtonpost.com/politics/ukraine-crisis-tests-obamas-foreign-policy-focus-on-diplomacy-over-military-force/2014/03/01/c83ec62c-a157-11e3-9ba6-800d1192d08b_story.html

The once-hopeful Arab Spring has staggered into civil war and military coup. China is stepping up territorial claims in the waters off East Asia. Longtime allies in Europe and in the Persian Gulf are worried by the inconsistency of a president who came to office promising the end of the United States' post-Sept. 11 wars.

The international response to protests in Ukraine intensified Saturday as Russia's parliament approved the use of the military to protect Russian interests in the politically-divided country.

Now Ukraine has emerged as a test of Obama's argument that, far from weakening American power, he has enhanced it through smarter diplomacy, stronger alliances and a realism untainted by the ideology that guided his predecessor."

It will be a hard argument for him to make, analysts say.

A measure of the drop in respect Obama has suffered is revealed in this accounting from the liberal Washington Post:

"Obama called Putin on Saturday[2] and expressed "deep concern over Russia's clear violation of Ukrainian sovereignty and territorial integrity, which is a breach of international law," the White House said.

---

[2]http://www.washingtonpost.com/world/national-security/us-and-allies-try-to-decide-on-response-to-ukraine-crisis/2014/03/01/463d1922-a174-11e3-b8d8-94577ff66b28_story.html

From a White House podium late Friday, Obama told the Russian government that "there will be costs"[3] for any military foray into Ukraine, including the semiautonomous region of Crimea, a strategically important peninsula on the Black Sea.

Within hours, Putin asked the Russian parliament for approval to send forces into Ukraine. The [vote] was unanimous, Obama's warning drowned out by lawmakers' rousing rendition of Russia's national anthem at the end of the session. Russian troops now control the Crimean Peninsula."

Putin has seen right through this sham of a man. Perhaps the Washington Post has also. If they have, they unlikely to be willing to share this knowledge unless it becomes necessary to protect their own reputation.

The position that America has put itself in regarding foreign affairs is disgraceful. It results from the naivete and utter incompetence of Obama and his administration. According to a different Washington Post article:[4]

"Obama said that a refusal by Russia to send troops back to their bases in Ukraine would "impact Russia's standing in the international community." According to the Kremlin, Putin argued that Ukrainian "ultranationalists" were threatening "the lives and health of Russian citizens" in Crimea.

On Sunday, Kerry said on NBC's "Meet the Press" that Putin is "going to lose on the international stage. Russia

---

[3]http://www.washingtonpost.com/blogs/post-politics/wp/2014/02/28/obama-warns-russia-on-ukraine/?hpid=z1

[4]http://www.washingtonpost.com/world/ukraines-leader-urges-putin-to-pull-back-military/2014/03/02/004ec166-a202-11e3-84d4-e59b1709222c_story.html

is going to lose, the Russian people are going to lose,
and he's going to lose all of the glow that came out of
the Olympics, his $60 billion extravaganza."

Kerry also said that the United States and its allies
would consider asset freezes, visa bans and trade penalties if Russian troops continued their incursion in
Crimea."

Does any of this sound like matters are improving? Kerry and
Obama are talkers. When talk is all you do, that is all you can do.

Republican Representative Mike Rogers characterized the Obama-
Putin confrontation better than most:

"Putin is playing chess, and I think we are playing
marbles and I don't think it's even close."

Apparently Obama did not bother to attend the National Security
briefing on this critical matter.

The weakness of Obama is obvious to all but our elected politicians.
World leaders are either scared (allies) or emboldened (foes) by
this man. Congress should man up and take some serious action to
prevent the continued destruction and endangerment of America.

IV SPECULATING ON THE ENDING

Barack Obama's phenomenal fall from grace continues, with no apparent sign of a bottom. His relationship with the American people has soured. His hard-core, "low-information" supporters still believe, but others have seen through the fraud. His drop in popularity and respect has potentially serious implications for his remaining time in office, **including the possibility that he may not complete his term**.

Deteriorating relationships with voters, Congress, the Democrat Party and the media increase the risk Obama faces. A host of alleged scandals make the situation particularly volatile and unstable. Any outcome could develop depending on new revelations pertaining to the scandals.

This section explores the importance of the 2014 mid-terms and the (still unlikely) possibility of impeachment proceedings.

A Turn For The Worse

Every presidency has its ebbs and flows. Few begin with the good will, expectations and popularity of Barack Obama. His entry into national politics was spectacular.

The recent announcement of a House Special Committee to investigate Benghazi increases the risks for the Obama Administration and those who have attempted to protect it. Contempt of Congress declared against a key player in the alleged IRS scandals is no minor matter either.

Other alleged scandals are potentially dangerous, but these two seem to present the biggest threat. Revelations in other areas could alter the importance of other issues.

Republicans appear to have been pushed to their limit in terms of stonewalling and obfuscation. Political motivations and advantage should never be discounted as motives for anything that happens in Washington. However, in advance of what looks like a big Republican victory in 2014 without investigations, it might not be politically wise to go on offensive prior to these results. The fact that they seem intent on doing just that says something. Although with Republicans it is often difficult to ascertain what.

These recent moves could simply reflect Republican stupidity. Or, they might indicate an increased concern over corrupt government. Unless there is something bigger and more sinister than is publicly known, moving now would seem to be politically stupid.

President Obama's Presidency Is At Risk

Republicans are known for both stupidity and cowardice. Making bold moves in advance of an election they appear destined to win and gain control of both Houses of Congress is certainly not cowardice. If there is no "there" there, then it is stupidity. If so, Republicans have ratcheted their stupidity to new and existential levels.

Are they that dumb? It would be nice to believe they are acting on principle, out of deep concern for the nation. That seems far-fetched unless the corruption and deceit is greater than the public currently comprehends.

If one assumes rationality on the part of Republicans, then we may be in the early stages of a series of significant events that lead to an impeachment proceeding.

Impeachment

The impeachment of a President is highly unusual. Rarely does Congress see fit to invoke Article II, section 4:

> The President, Vice President and all civil Officers of the United States, shall be removed from Office on Impeachment for, and Conviction of, Treason, Bribery, or other high Crimes and Misdemeanors.

Should impeachment occur (and it is not yet predicted), it would likely fall under the amorphous "high Crimes and Misdemeanors" category. There is no formal legal definition for this phrase. Nor is there meaningful precedent to define it.

An impeachment movement is always more political than legal. Considerations of this issue appear in this part of the book.

37 The Impeachment Issue

MARCH 4, 2014

The question of the day, at least in my mind, was the question of the day four years ago: **When will the Democrats turn on Barack Obama?**

Even the most cynical among us regarding political ethics and integrity know there is some point when the supporters turn and run. Bruce Bialosky[1] discussed this issue in an excellent piece:

> We are all guilty of providing a wide leeway to a politician that we favor. If the politician is someone we support, we restrain ourselves when something becomes public that would have us in a tizzy if done by someone with whom we dislike politically. That is referred to as "cutting someone some slack." But there is a limit for everyone like there was for Anthony Weiner or Larry Craig. When will the grownups in the Democratic Party say enough is enough with Barack Obama?

We may be closer to this point than the media dare acknowledge.

37.1 How Bad Is It?

It is very bad if you are a Democrat up for election. Here are some of the reasons why:

---

[1]http://www.jewishworldreview.com/0314/bialosky.php3#.UxW9sEpZ9a4

1. There is no economic recovery; nor will there be one given Obama's policies.

2. ObamaCare is a disaster, acknowledged as such by many of its supporters, especially those most vulnerable to voter wrath. Creatures will continue to crawl out from under rocks as this monstrosity unfolds.

3. Obama is now ready to present a budget that claims his first five years represented "austerity." He apparently has a different view of austerity than most. He believes it is time for government to begin spending again. **Wow!** One wonders how the debt got so high with low spending. Delusional is a word that comes to mind regarding this belief.

4. "Tyranny" is increasingly used to describe Obama's style of governance. His branch of the government assumes itself more equal than the other two branches, an attitude that troubles the other two branches. He did not think this way until he became president.

5. Scandal fatigue is another serious problem. No other Administration has been so embroiled in the number, magnitude and constitutionally-pertinent scandals. No other Administration has "stonewalled" investigations like this one. Richard Nixon was threatened with impeachment and resigned over what looks like jaywalking in retrospect. Forty-year old ethics (which weren't much when Nixon held office) would have forced impeachment talk in Obama's first term.

6. Internationally the world doubts whether the US can be trusted. Long-term allies distance themselves; long-term enemies are emboldened. Obama's kumbaya version of diplomacy has been an utter failure. Realpolitik has overpowered his fantasy-land vision.

America has never been held in less esteem by the international community. Obama now ranks behind the hapless Jimmy Carter in terms of international respect. The world is substantially more dangerous as a result of his leadership ("leadership" is probably not a good word to use in the same paragraph with "Obama").

37.2 Is It Bad Enough?

As Democrats approach a potential Waterloo election, political self-interest and survival might cause them to force a Weiner, Craig or Nixon moment upon Barack Obama. For several years I believed that would occur and that it would have happened by now. Obviously I overestimated the low level of integrity in Washington. I was wrong and four reasons now influence my opinion:

1. The Democrat Party has no easy solution to their problem. Having this President impeached is the right thing to do, given the Constitutional and (potentially) criminal violations that have occurred. That action would create an enormous blot on the Party that would linger for years. "Kicking this can down the road" is a way of not incurring that damage all at once. From a political (not ethical or legal) standpoint that is probably the easiest way out. After all, the albatross is gone in about three years.

2. I suspect, without evidence, that the White House has information on every power player in Washington as a result of NSA monitoring. Most, if not all, of these powerful men and women have scandals, illegalities or other hidden improprieties. The NSA probably already has this information. Congressmen that fit this category are easily dissuaded (blackmailed) from creating problems for the President. One wonders whether this tactic was used against General Petraeus, Chief Justice Roberts or others. The large numbers of high-ranking military removed from office without objection lends additional support to this speculation.

3. Even if the prior point is false, Obama believes that he is "above the law." So too do many in the Washington elite. It is

doubtful that a Congressional delegation providing a "go to Nixon" meeting would penetrate Obama's delusions.

4. The case for impeachment runs up against the hourglass of time. There is a point when the process itself exceeds the time (and risks) remaining in Obama's term. There is a point where Congress has their Hillary moment and exclaims: What difference does it make!? He is gone in – a month, a year, two years.

Mr. Bialosky ends his piece with the following:

"It is time for Democrats to stand and say no more. If you don't do it now there could be permanent harm to our democracy. Certainly some of you will no longer be in office come this November because the American people will certainly say enough is enough."

Sadly, it was time before this to say "no more." It wasn't done then and it may not be done now unless there is some piece of evidence that is so egregious that the Democrats will judge it more costly to not act than to act. The political calculus is simple and has nothing to do with integrity or ethics. If Democrats consider Obama, figuratively, worth more dead than alive, they will move against him. It all involves their perception of what they judge is best for themselves.

That unfortunately is the state of our democracy. Political ignorance has already permanently harmed it. An informed electorate would never have elected this man in the first place, and certainly not twice!

38 Falling Apart

MARCH 16, 2014

It is falling apart for President Obama. His fall from grace is difficult to overestimate. The totality of his failure and the ramifications of his fall have not yet been fully appreciated nor played out. Things are going to get worse.

Political supporters are abandoning him, disillusioned to learn that there was nothing behind the facade that propelled him to office. For a while it appeared as though he could do no wrong. Now he can do nothing right and he is increasingly viewed as incompetent, ineffective and not to be trusted. Nowhere is the angst greater than among Democrats up for election.

Maureen Dowd[1], a true Liberal, commented on the fall of The One:

> "Hill Democrats are seething at Obama, fearing that the onetime messiah is putting them in a slough that will last until, or through, 2016.
>
> Top Democrats who were fans of the president and prone to giving him the benefit of the doubt now say they've completely lost confidence in the White House's ability to advance an agenda and work with them in a way that's going to give Democrats a fighting chance in November."

[1] http://www.nytimes.com/2014/03/16/opinion/sunday/dowd-dems-in-distress.html?_r=0

The anger and fear among Democrats is palpable. Sadly this anger is not precipitated by any concern for the country but purely self-interest. Those who risk being tossed from the trough are the most worried.

Obama is not a typical Democrat. He is personally hard to like. He did not pay his dues like other politicians. His success was and is viewed by other politicians as a fluke. There was nothing in his background other than an Elmer Gantry style that suggested he could become president. Nor was there anything to suggest he was qualified for the office. (Just what is a community organizer other than an Al Sharpton before he tried to go legit?).

None of this mattered when Obama could advance Democrat causes and individual careers. Don't question how or what happened, merely accept and exploit this Democrat manna from Heaven.

But now it is over. Obama is increasingly seen as a fraud. He is a liability. Democrats running for re-election don't want to be seen with him. He is considered toxic.

It is a dangerous time for this Flimflam Man. He has no friends in Washington, a pattern that seems to have characterized his entire life. None of the power brokers care about him, only what he can do for or to them. Now, he can no longer help them.

When this website began more than four years ago, this outcome was predicted. To be fair, my timing was awful. I expected the turn against Obama to occur in his first term. I never expected him to get re-elected. Apparently, I did something that H. L. Mencken abhorred: I underestimated the stupidity of the electorate and the Republican opposition.

39 Politics Loves Winners And Hates Losers

MARCH 19, 2014

Politics loves winners and hates losers. Winners are loved because they can be used to advance a cause or a career. Losers are useless and rejected as soon as they are recognized as such. **Politics abandons its wounded.**

Barack Obama was a winner, an extraordinary one. He is now a loser, and just as extraordinary a one. The Democrats have little more use for him, but are bound to him like a prisoner is to a ball and chain. They would like to abandon him but may not have the means to do so that don't redound unfavorably on them and their brand.

What began as a great American success is ending like a Greek tragedy. Charles Dicken's "A Tale of Two Cities" opens with perhaps the best-known introduction to any novel:

> **It was the best of times, it was the worst of times, it was the age of wisdom, it was the age of foolishness**

This lead might be appropriate at the beginning of a tale of the last couple of decades in American politics. These words, slightly modified, aptly describe our two most recent presidents:

> It was the best of men, it was the worst of men

Neither truly ranks at either extreme, but Obama and Bush are polar opposites with regard to ethics, integrity, personality and policy. The passage of time is necessary to make definitive judgments, but some observations are useful.

39.1 George W. Bush

George W. Bush was portrayed as an idiot by the Left, as was Ronald Reagan before him. Attack the man and not the idea is a technique as old as politics. It avoids real issues.

Whatever George W. Bush's IQ (supposedly it was higher than most Democrats he battled against), he had prior managerial experience. He was mostly respected around the world (contrary to what the Left wanted you to believe).

The word "humble" was a word that could describe him, even if it were followed by detractors adding one of their favorite pejoratives, "cowboy." Bush's standing grows as the current world situation deteriorates (but then so does Jimmy Carter's).

Bush took pride in serving the country. He respected the office and never blamed his predecessor or others for his situation. He was likable and seemed decent, regardless of what you thought of his politics.

There were things to like and dislike about Bush's time in office. History will eventually flush these out. Regarding his intelligence (whatever that word is supposed to mean), it seems that he had an adequate amount to properly handle the job.

39.2 Barack Obama

When Barack Obama won in 2008, the Left believed they had elected their "Messiah." Obama promoted and encouraged this image.

Obama is no longer worshiped. Hunter Thompson's phrase, "fear and loathing" seems more applicable today. Former supporters and many Democrats run from him. An appearance with him is considered toxic for anyone running for office.

Many on the Left see through Obama now. The rest of the world, less subject to filtered news from our still clueless and fawning US media, focuses on policies not persona. Many of Obama's policies are incomprehensible to allies and enemies. Allies wish for the good old days when a "cowboy" was in the saddle.

The international community admired Obama's style, initially. Now, they wonder how America could have elected such a man. His performance affects them as well as America.

Obama appears incapable of anything other than sounding good (with a teleprompter) while telling lies. The halo is gone and many former faithful see the man for what he is – an outright fraud! **He has no qualifications, no abilities and no ethics**.

Obama is the walking embodiment of the derogatory phrase: "talk is cheap." He is the polar opposite of Teddy Roosevelt. Obama believes in talking loudly and carrying no stick.

When you are a self-anointed Messiah, talking about something seems adequate. Plans, programs and execution aren't needed. Words make things happen. The mention of something is considered a solution.

According to Dwight Kehoe[1], the following list of absurdities had to be overlooked by the media, the Democrat Party, the Republican Party and a majority of the voters to allow Obama to ascend to office:

- "He was allowed to hide his academic records, from grammar school through college.
- He was allowed to fabricate a life history which included made up girlfriends and authorship of books.

---

[1] http://www.tpath.org/COMMENTARY_2014.php#HisLies

- He was allowed to forge Selective Service documents.
- He was allowed to use a Social Security number not issued to him.
- He was allowed to hide the fact that all his mentors were communists and haters of America.
- He was allowed to hide his passport records and his travel to Islamic countries.
- He was allowed to forge a birth certificate in order to prove the un-provable.
- He was allowed to run for the office of the Presidency despite his Constitutional ineligibility.
- He was allowed to run for the most difficult, important job in the world without a bit of experience.
- And most important of all, he was supported by the media and his political party even though they knew he was a compulsive and habitual liar incapable of uttering the truth about his past or his intentions."

People invested heavily in this man. Many of them now find their own futures in jeopardy.

39.3 A Tale of Two Men

Bush and Obama are very different. Bush was humble; Obama arrogant. Bush accepted responsibility; Obama blames others. Bush was unpretentious and not aloof; Obama is just the opposite.

I don't recall other world leaders openly mocking George W. Bush like Vladimir Putin has done with Obama. Putin called out the fraud in the White House, something that our media and Congress has been unwilling to do. Perhaps Putin should demand Obama's Nobel Prize for his service in exposing our charlatan. Putin's ridicule might serve to wake up those in the media and others who were cowed or awed by Obama.

39.4 Hubris

It is dangerous to be arrogant, even if you are the smartest man in the room. There are always other rooms and other people. No one will always be the smartest. **Arrogance when it is accompanied with incompetence is stupidity of the highest order** and usually fatal.

We have reached the stage of Obama's career that will be classified as tragic. Merriam-Webster[2] defines tragedy as follows:

> "Drama of a serious and dignified character that typi-cally describes the development of a conflict between the protagonist and a superior force (such as destiny, circumstance, or society) and reaches a sorrowful or disastrous conclusion."

Barack Obama is finished, although he and his minions don't recognize this terminal condition. He has probably destroyed the Democrat Party for a generation. Tragically, he does not understand that he no longer commands respect. Fear is his only remaining tool and that is disappearing also.

Obama is viewed by increasing numbers as a public nuisance. His style of speaking no longer works, it annoys. Hot air can be peddled and recycled for only so long.

This tragedy has three more years to unfold. As a dilettante of aberrant psychology, I will enjoy watching this tragi-comedy play out. As a man who loves this country, I abhor what is happening.

---

[2]http://www.merriam-webster.com/dictionary/tragedy

40 Bully Meets Professional Bully

APRIL 17, 2014

What happens when the biggest bully around gets confronted by someone who refuses to be bullied? Usually the bully backs down and avoids the confrontation. But what happens if the one who confronted him is himself a bully? **What happens if he won't allow the other to back down?**

That scenario may be the one playing out between Barack Obama and Vladimir Putin. Obama is the first bully and Putin the second. Ukraine provides a convenient venue for Putin to ridicule and embarrass the man Putin considers all form and no substance.

40.1 Vlad and Barry

Vladimir Putin is hardly a perfect man. There is little to like about him. His history and his methods are those of the old Soviet Union. He competed, survived and thrived in the rough and tumble world of the KGB. He was tested and hardened by that process. He understands the cost of being wrong.

He is a tough no-nonsense guy who believes the Soviet Union must rise again. He achieved and won in competitive environments most of us probably don't want to imagine. Putin is a man of substance even though his methods or achievements may not be pleasant or admirable.

Barack Obama is also imperfect. He is everything that Putin is not. He has never been tested. His life has been soft and pampered. His position was not achieved via accomplishment or ability, unless you confuse fooling a majority of Mencken's "booboise" with ability. Obama lacks substance, qualifications and experience. He is weak. And he is arrogant.

Weakness combined with arrogance is a dangerous combination. To a man like Putin, the former is to be exploited. Arrogance, when not backed up with ability, likely only increases Putin's animosity.

Obama represents everything that Putin detests. Personal relations between the two men are non-existent, which is apparent in joint appearances. Putin resents having to deal with what he considers a weak, overbearing phony.

No one doubts who would win in a martial arts contest between the two men. That is not going to happen, but that doesn't mean that Putin will not find other ways to humiliate, perhaps destroy, his opponent.

Obama is the bully who was called out. He wants to leave the scene, but Putin is a bigger bully who wants to publicly dismantle him. The boy who pretends to be tough has met the man who really is tough. The professional bully is out to expose the pretender. Putin is unwilling to let Obama retreat.

40.2 Bullies or Sociopaths?

Richard Fernandez[1] has a slightly different take on what is going on between Obama and Putin. He describes it this way:

> "Obama has been yelling 'stop! stop!' and still Putin is twisting his arm. The president made yet another plea to Putin according to Carol Lee in the Wall Street

---

[1]http://pjmedia.com/richardfernandez/2014/04/15/sadist-versus-narcissist/#more-36053

Journal[2]: "White House Tells Kremlin Diplomacy Is Still an Option Despite Escalation". Putin is making Obama crawl to lick his boots."

Mr. Fernandez did not use the bully analogy. He believes the contest is better described as one between a narcissist and a sadist:

> "One reason why Putin has made a special effort to humiliate the president is that his profilers may have pegged Obama as suffering from narcissistic personality disorder. Putin the secret policeman must be thinking: how do you get a narcissist to melt down? Answer: by personally and publicly shaming him, thereby provoking a narcissistic rage[3].

> That rage can take either of two forms: a reckless act or a withdrawal into a fantasy in which the narcissist remains invincible in some universe of his own."

The narcissistic disorder that plagues Obama has been speculated about openly. Putin has access to experts and strategists that laymen do not. He has geopolitical as well as personal motives to exploit what he considers a weak and undeserving leader, especially one who foolishly believes himself to be superior to all others?

Regardless of what happens in Ukraine, it is a sideshow to the personal interplay between these two men. Obama is in this game, whether he wants to be or not. He is the hunted and not the hunter. Putin is unlikely to stop before he gets what he wants. At the moment that seems to be the complete humiliation of Barack Obama. Geographical gains are just an added bonus.

---

[2] http://online.wsj.com/news/articles/SB10001424052702303663604579500971938538690
[3] http://en.wikipedia.org/wiki/Narcissistic_rage_and_narcissistic_injury

Americans should be grateful for Putin. He provides a public service to those who voted for our mountebank. He exposes the empty suit that sits in the White House. He is doing the job that the media should have done six years ago.

On the other hand, games played by sociopaths (the jury is still out on Putin's classification) can spin out of control. When Obama calls "Uncle" and Putin refuses to acknowledge his surrender, what then happens? Does Obama give away strategic assets or fly into a rage that precipitates something that should never occur?

Our man-child does not appear stable. Putin knows that.

This personality clash may not end well. The US representative is seriously over matched.

41 Democrats Turn on King Cnut

APRIL 30, 2014

America's version of King Cnut, Barack Obama, is coming under fire.

For those unfamiliar with Cnut, J. P. Sommerville[1] provided this brief description:

> Canute's (Cnut's) name is known nowadays largely because of the story that he was so proud that he thought his command could hold back the tide.

Barack Obama, a modern version of Cnut The Great,[2] believes he can command and his desired outcomes will magically occur. After five years, it now seems that even many of the Kool-Aid imbibers have seen through this act. Domestic and foreign policy are in shambles.

In my lifetime, no president has presided over (created!) worse conditions in either area. None had the talent to bring down both at the same time, except Jimmy Carter. Arguably, Obama's legacy is apt to be that he out-Cartered Carter.

Obama is a liability. He is an albatross who threatens Democrats individually and collectively. His near total failure in the job has jeopardized Democrats who believed they had lifetime sinecure. The 2014 election has become an existential event for many of them.

---

[1]http://faculty.history.wisc.edu/sommerville/123/Canute%20Waves.htm
[2]http://en.wikipedia.org/wiki/Cnut_the_Great

Those threatened will do anything to survive. Wes Pruden said it well:[3]

> **You can't expect a senator to worry about a soon-to-be ex-president's legacy when his own survival is at stake. Going back to Nome or Fairbanks to look for a job is an awful prospect. Besides, the president should have thought about his legacy when he was making one. **

Those who enjoy the madness that accompanies political elections are in for a special treat. Disciples of Obama now act as Peter from the gospels:

> "Peter replied, "Even if all fall away on account of you, I never will." "I tell you the truth," Jesus answered, "This very night, before the rooster crows, you will disown me three times." But Peter declared, "Even if I have to die with you, I will never disown you." And all the other disciples said the same."Source[4]

Of course Peter denied Jesus just as many Obama supporters will deny Obama. Peter came back. Most of Obama's supporters will not. Some will become Judas.

How many Democrat politicians will turn? How Will Obama's fragile psyche hold up if he is rejected by his own Party? Both questions are likely to be answered with the passage of time. The second one is especially important. An imbalanced man with a Red Button can do great harm.

We are watching great political theater. The drama will intensify as the 2014 election nears. Watch the sub-plots, identify the Peters and watch how Obama reacts to the pressure.

---

[3]http://www.jewishworldreview.com/cols/pruden042914.php3#.U2A_5PldV7E
[4]http://en.wikipedia.org/wiki/Denial_of_Peter

Where is H. L. Mencken when needed? Someone with his cynical insight could properly frame and appreciate this tragi-farce. No one did it better than H. L., who is probably enjoying a beer and cigar contentedly watching the madness he knew was inevitable.

42 A Whiff of Impeachment

MAY 5, 2014

Do I think impeachment is in the air? Yes. Do I think it will happen? Probably not, but the odds are moving in the wrong direction for the Obama Administration. Recently this trend accelerated to the point where a likely scenario is imaginable.

42.1 Why Impeachment Is So Difficult

Impeachment is defined in Article 2, Section 4 of the Constitution:

> "The President, Vice President and all civil Officers of the United States, shall be removed from Office on Impeachment for, and Conviction of, Treason, Bribery, or other high Crimes and Misdemeanors."

Treason, bribery or other high crimes and misdemeanors must be present. A few comments regarding these conditions:

- Bribery, other than what we call campaign contributions, is no longer an issue at the presidential level. Anyone who holds the office is literally able to define his own wealth after his term is up. Outrageous speaking fees provide much of the revenue and would be called bribery if accepted while in office. They become acceptable out of office. In reality, these and other emoluments are little more than deferred payments for privileges formerly granted. They are settlement of implied IOUs.

- Treason is a difficult charge to even understand these days. Ed Snowden qualifies according to some. Others think not. Without defined enemies (we fight nations and against many groups but not under any declaration of war) can you actually aid and abet an enemy. Treason is more broadly defined than that, although probably not for a president.
- High crimes and misdemeanors have never been formally defined. Like pornography, they are hard to define but supposedly easy to know when seen.

High crimes and misdemeanors is a catch-all category. Republicans probably see many violations in this area while Democrats do not. Is lying to the American public in virtually every public appearance a high crime or misdemeanor? Bill Clinton lied under sworn testimony and skated. Why would lying not under oath, regardless of how frequently, qualify? Or, why would lying under oath not qualify?

Issues like these show why it is so hard to bring impeachment proceedings against a sitting president. Legal proceedings usually turn on black letter law, but not impeachment.

42.2 The Rule of Men

The United States was founded on the principle of the rule of law as opposed to the rule of men. Arguably the impeachment clause in the Constitution was based more on the rule of men, possibly because of the difficulty in defining impeachable conduct. The Founders were precise in other areas of the Constitution. Ambiguity or room for interpretation was likely intended here.

Impeachment is always a political act. Politicians determine whether to begin an action and politicians rule on the case. Impeachment proceedings are not brought against popular presidents, although Republicans did not seem to understand that when they took on the popular Bill Clinton. Andrew Johnson came within one vote of being removed from office while Richard Nixon resigned rather than face almost certain conviction. Both presidents were unpopular.

Impeaching Barack Obama, regardless of his actions or policies, was unthinkable during his first term. When he entered office his approval ratings were so high that had he been caught on tape murdering someone, Congress probably would not have had the courage to impeach. (Hopefully criminal law would have been enforced.)

The shield of popularity that Obama began with has become awfully thin and flimsy.

42.3 Why Obama Might Be Impeached

Regardless of how serious the so-called smoking-gun Benghazi memo appears, it is not enough to produce a call for impeachment. It is, however, reason to dig deeper as it shows an attempt to deceive.

The Benghazi memo provided a catalyst that most Americans can relate to. The memo confirmed many people's suspicions that they were lied to. It appears as though the internet video never mattered other than as cover for Administration ineptness.

Obama lies routinely. The lies are so frequent and often so mundane that they seem unnecessary and foolish. That Benghazi should be any different, despite four American deaths, would be surprising.

The blatant attempt to blame Benghazi on a video when that story was implausible, may have crossed a threshold that even Obama supporters cannot condone. A US Ambassador was murdered along with three others. Witnesses were not allowed to testify, even those involved and wounded in the incident. No one has been brought to justice.

Benghazi smelled like a cover up from the beginning. The memo only made the odor worse. The abundance of other potential scandals does not help this Administration's credibility. According to Keith Koffler, there are at least twenty-four Obama scandals:[1]

> **1. IRS targets Obama's enemies:** The IRS targeted conservative and pro-Israel groups prior to the 2012 election. Questions are being raised about why this occurred, who ordered it, whether there was any White House involvement and whether there was an initial effort to hide who knew about the targeting and when.

> **2. Benghazi:** This is actually three scandals in one: - The failure of administration to protect the Benghazi mission. - The changes made to the talking points in order to suggest the attack was motivated by an anti-Muslim video. - The refusal of the White House to say what President Obama did the night of the attack.

> **3. Watching the AP:** The Justice Department performed a massive cull of Associated Press reporters' phone records as part of a leak investigation.

> **4. Rosengate:** The Justice Department suggested that Fox News reporter James Rosen is a criminal for reporting about classified information and subsequently monitored his phones and emails.

> **5. Potential Holder perjury I:** Attorney General Eric Holder told Congress he had never been associated with "potential prosecution" of a journalist for perjury when in fact he signed the affidavit that termed Rosen a potential criminal.

---

[1] http://www.whitehousedossier.com/2013/08/01/obama-dozen-scandals-counting/

6. The ATF "Fast and Furious" scheme: Allowed weapons from the U.S. to "walk" across the border into the hands of Mexican drug dealers. The ATF lost track of hundreds of firearms, many of which were used in crimes, including the December 2010 killing of Border Patrol Agent Brian Terry.

7. Potential Holder Perjury II: Holder told Congress in May 2011 that he had just recently heard about the Fast and Furious gun walking scheme when there is evidence he may have known much earlier.

8. Sebelius demands payment: HHS Secretary Kathleen Sebelius solicited donations from companies HHS might regulate. The money would be used to help her sign up uninsured Americans for ObamaCare.

9. The Pigford scandal: An Agriculture Department effort that started as an attempt to compensate black farmers who had been discriminated against by the agency but evolved into a gravy train delivering several billion dollars in cash to thousands of additional minority and female farmers who probably didn't face discrimination.

10. GSA gone wild: The General Services Administration in 2010 held an $823,000 training conference in Las Vegas, featuring a clown and a mind readers. Resulted in the resignation of the GSA administrator.

11. Veterans Affairs in Disney World: The agency wasted more than $6 million on two conferences in Orlando. An assistant secretary was fired.

12. Sebelius violates the Hatch Act: A U.S. special counsel determined that Sebelius violated the Hatch Act when she made "extemporaneous partisan remarks" during a speech in her official capacity last year. During the remarks, Sebelius called for the election of the Democratic candidate for governor of North Carolina.

13. Solyndra: Republicans charged the Obama administration funded and promoted its poster boy for green energy despite warning signs the company was headed for bankruptcy. The administration also allegedly pressed Solyndra to delay layoff announcements until after the 2010 midterm elections.

14. AKA Lisa Jackson: Former EPA Administrator Lisa Jackson used the name "Richard Windsor" when corresponding by email with other government officials, drawing charges she was trying to evade scrutiny.

15. The New Black Panthers: The Justice Department was accused of using a racial double standard in failing to pursue a voter intimidation case against Black Panthers who appeared to be menacing voters at a polling place in 2008 in Philadelphia.

16. Waging war all by myself: Obama may have violated the Constitution and both the letter and the spirit of the War Powers Resolution by attacking Libya without Congressional approval.

17. Biden bullies the press: Vice President Biden's office has repeatedly interfered with coverage, including forcing a reporter to wait in a closet, making a reporter delete photos, and editing pool reports.

18. AKPD not A-OK: The administration paid millions to the former firm of then-White House adviser David Axelrod, AKPD Message and Media, to promote passage of Obamacare. Some questioned whether the firm was hired to help pay Axelrod $2 million AKPD owed him.

19. Sestak, we'll take care of you: Former White House Chief of Staff Rahm Emanuel used Bill Clinton as an intermediary to probe whether former Rep. Joe Sestak (D-Pa.) would accept a prominent, unpaid White House advisory position in exchange for dropping out of the 2010 primary against former Sen. Arlen Specter (D-Pa.).

20. I'll pass my own laws: Obama has repeatedly been accused of making end runs around Congress by deciding which laws to enforce, including the decision not to deport illegal immigrants who may have been allowed to stay in the United States had Congress passed the "Dream Act."

21. The hacking of Sharyl Attkisson's computer: It's not clear who hacked the CBS reporter's computer as she investigated the Benghazi scandal, but the Obama administration and its allies had both the motive and the means to do it.

22. An American Political Prisoner: The sudden decision to arrest Nakoula Basseley Nakoula on unrelated charges after protests in the Arab world over his anti-Muslim video is an extraordinarily suspicious coincidence. "We're going to go out and we're going to prosecute the person that made that video," Hillary

Clinton allegedly told the father of one of the ex-SEALs killed in Benghazi.

23. Get rid of inconvenient IGs: Corporation for National and Community Service Inspector General Gerald Walpin was fired in 2009 as he fought wasteful spending and investigated a friend of Obama's, Sacramento Mayor and former NBA player Kevin Johnson. The White House says Walpin was incompetent.

24. Influence peddling: An investigation is underway of Alejandro Mayorkas, director of the U.S. Citizenship and Immigration Services, who has been nominated by Obama for the number two post at the Department of Homeland Security. Mayorkas may have used his position to unfairly obtain U.S. visas for foreign investors in company run by Hillary Clinton's brother, Anthony Rodman.

Even if 90% of these are bogus (i.e., not impeachable offenses) there is serious reason for concern. The list itself was compiled more than six months ago, offering the potential for new additions before Obama's second term ends.

[The VA scandal is now breaking as is the release of five key terrorists in exchange for what appears to have been a confused American deserter. These two bring the total to 26.]

42.4 Obama's Popularity is Plummeting

The risk for Obama is that his popularity continues to decline and with it the Democrat brand. The Pew organization, hardly a right-wing operation, released some findings which seem devastating for Obama and Democrats. Table I shows three different April data points. They are from 2006, 2010 and 2014, respectively. April 2006 measures George W. Bush at or near his low-point in popularity.

Challenging Midterm Landscape for Democrats

Based on registered voters

	April 2006	March 2010	April 2014
Midterm vote	%	%	%
Rep/Lean Rep	41	44	47
Dem/Lean Dem	51	44	43
Other/Don't know	8	12	9
	100	100	100

Think of vote as for or against the president?	April 2006	Feb 2010	April 2014
For the president	17	24	16
Against the president	34	20	26
President not much of a factor	46	51	54
	3	5	4
	100	100	100

Survey conducted April 23-27, 2014.
Figures may not add to 100% because of rounding.

PEW RESEARCH CENTER/USA TODAY

Table I

The top half of Table I shows the generic Democrat-Republic polling. Even when Republicans win mid-term elections they rarely lead in the generic polling. This type of polling tends to overstate Democrat strength. If that holds true, the readings above suggest the upcoming mid-terms may rival the wave of 2010.

Table II shows the drop in "pull" or "coattail effect" provided by Obama. The reluctance of Democrats up for election to be seen with Obama suggest they already know the potential adverse reaction.

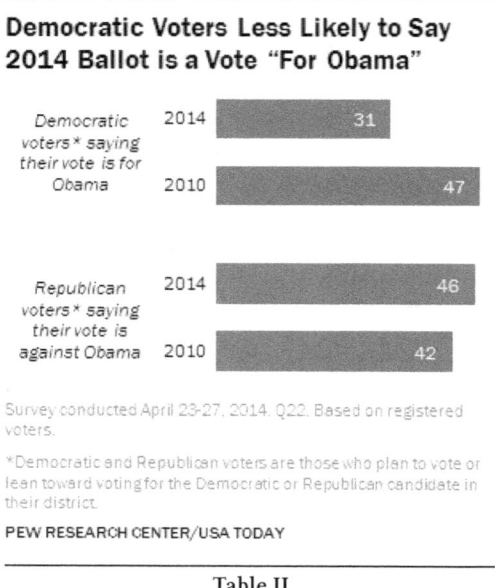

Democratic Voters Less Likely to Say 2014 Ballot is a Vote "For Obama"

Survey conducted April 23-27, 2014. Q22. Based on registered voters.

*Democratic and Republican voters are those who plan to vote or lean toward voting for the Democratic or Republican candidate in their district.

PEW RESEARCH CENTER/USA TODAY

Table II

Popularity sets the threshold for impeachment probabilities. As popularity declines that threshold comes closer to being crossed. The trend is not a good one for Obama. Yet even when the threshold is met, there still must be evidence of "high crimes and misdemeanors."

42.5 Obama's Developing Media Problem

If this polling data were all that there were, it is unlikely Republicans would dare bring impeachment proceedings (short of another smoking gun relative to Benghazi or one of the other alleged scandals).

The media appears to be wary of the situation and its potential to become more serious. Howard Kurtz[2] notes:

> "The press has turned on President Obama with a vengeance."

Whether it be a full-turn or only a CYA one (I suspect the latter), the once Kool-Aid guzzling media are now positioning themselves in case Ship Obama begins to sink. They are unwilling to go down with it and are setting the stage to mutiny should it be necessary. There were indications prior to the Benghazi memo. (David Brooks famously questioning Obama's manhood was one of many examples). Now doubts about Obama are openly discussed, even among strong media supporters.

Economic and foreign policy became harder for media disciples to defend. ObamaCare makes more enemies with the passage of time and as more unpleasant surprises are discovered. Nothing Obama has done can be pointed to as positive unless you believe driving millions of productive Americans to food stamps and other welfare assistance is a good thing.

In short, the media cannot defend Obama without risking their own dwindling credibility. Obama's failure has eclipsed that of the hapless Jimmy Carter. We know where Carter bottomed out. Obama is still dropping. The media may have to drop the sponsorship of "their" guy.

Without media protection, more of the brain-dead followers will abandon Obama, presumably by staying home for the mid-terms.

42.6 The Democrat Shoe

Arguably, a case for impeachment proceedings could be made. However, it is still fantasy to believe that matters have progressed far enough to wisely do so.

---

[2]http://www.cnn.com/2013/05/17/opinion/kurtz-obama-ap-scandal/

The 2014 mid-terms could change that overnight. If the Democrat defeat is as big as some predict, the Senate will change hands. Talk would turn to whether the Democrat Party has a future.

Many Democrat careers will have ended abruptly. The party will be in ruin, either destroyed in terms of liberalism or resigned to the shadows for a decade or so. Those who survive will disassociate themselves with the perceived cause – Barack Obama. Some may even consider it smart politics to push for Obama's impeachment.

One hopes that both Republicans and Democrats would act responsibly in the event that impeachment becomes a movement. The political balance of power would have shifted, but political advantage should not influence anything so important. Unfortunately, neither political party seems capable of behaving responsibly.

Before this piece of political history ends, Democrats may rue Obama more than Republicans.

43 Does The Administration Consider Impeachment Possible?

MAY 8, 2014

Two days ago a post entitled Whiff of Impeachment[1] addressed the increasing potential for the impeachment of President Barack Obama.

That post was not intended as a prediction. Impeachment is an unusually rare occurrence. That post explored how the once unthinkable could become possible. Recent and expected future events like the results of the 2014 mid-terms, were discussed in terms of their effects on altering the probabilities of such an occurrence.

An interesting sub-plot that was not discussed is President Obama's pathological narcissism. Is he capable of recognizing that his popularity has decreased and his vulnerability increased? His continued "pen and phone" threats and executive orders to bypass Congress suggest he does not, at least at this point.

Given Obama's drop in popularity and increasing potential for legal issues, it would seem foolish to continue to try to diminish and invalidate Congress. Continued taunting indicates supreme confidence, confidence that seems to be rooted in Obama's personality disorders rather than emerging realities.

Obama's ego may prevent him from accepting such possibilities, but the halcyon "messiah days" which he milked for all they were worth, are gone and will not return. It is impossible to determine

---

[1]http://www.economicnoise.com/?p=48944

whether his apparent confidence reflects bluster and bravado or, whether like an over-the-hill actor, he continues to play a role that he is no longer suited for.

To paraphrase Ayn Rand, Obama can ignore reality but reality is not going to ignore him. Nor is Congress. Congress is filled with over-inflated egos, some bigger than Obama's. Taunting these people only creates animosity on both sides of the aisle.

Despite Obama's bravado, someone appears to grasp the growing risk. The time line below, described by M. Catherine Evans[2], supports that:

> "Judicial Watch has fought for two years to get documents from the State Departments specifically pertaining to the talking points used by former U.N. Ambassador Susan Rice on talk shows. A federal judge finally ordered their release two weeks ago. Three days later, Obama hired Eggleston. Eight days later, JW went public with the e-mails.

Is this a coincidence? Don't personnel changes routinely occur among higher-level staff? Perhaps, but Neil Eggleston is an interesting pick given his background. Ms. Evans provided this background:

> Politico[3] reported on the switch and made mention of Eggleston's role in the Whitewater investigation during Clinton's first term, as well as his ties to Obama's former White House chief of staff, Rahm Emanuel. The high-powered lawyer helped Emanuel avoid jail time in the pay-to-play schemes involving former Illinois governor Rod Blagojevich.

---

[2]http://www.americanthinker.com/blog/2014/05/was_obama_hiring_of_criminal_lawyer_due_to_benghazi_emails.html

[3]http://www.politico.com/story/2014/04/w-neil-eggleston-white-house-counsel-105869.html

> Politico then suggested that Obama needed Eggleston in case of a GOP sweep in November.
>
> Eggleston is a partner at Kirkland & Ellis and has extensive experience in the kinds of oversight cases that the Obama White House is likely to face more of if Republicans take control of the Senate in November and retain control of the House."

The move, coincidental or not, seems appropriate for what could be a rapidly deteriorating situation.

President Obama probably did not engineer this personnel change, although he obviously approved it. Narcissism and his ego likely prevented him (and possibly still do) from considering the possibility of impeachment. Valerie Jarrett whose job it is to protect the President likely initiated the move.

If there is more than a coincidence associated with the timing and choice of Eggleston, there may be bigger problems forthcoming. Those responsible for the personnel change know what monsters reside behind the closed doors they protect so faithfully.

Blogger George Washington[4] clearly believes there is more and discusses these issues in the linked article.

Stay tuned. Hopefully Congress pursues the alleged scandals to definitive conclusions. The time for politics should be over, although it rarely ever is.

---

[4]http://www.zerohedge.com/contributed/2014-05-07/4-deeper-truths-about-benghazi-and-libya

44 Albatross Politics – Democrats Have A Problem

MAY 9, 2014

Albatrosses are always in season, at least in politics. No hunting license is required and all weapons are legal.

44.1 What Is An Albatross?

The albatross is a bird but the term here is used metaphorically. In this sense, it refers to a heavy burden. Its origin comes from an old poem. Here is a relevant passage:

> Ah ! well a-day ! what evil looks
> Had I from old and young !
> Instead of the cross, the Albatross About my neck was hung.

The passage is from Samuel Taylor Coleridge's[1] poem The Rime of the Ancient Mariner[2] (1798). The albatross metaphor describes the deteriorating relationship between the Democrat Party and their one-time superstar, Barack Obama.

Recent posts dealt with the likelihood of impeachment (here[3] and here[4]). These indicated that impeachment was not yet probable but that developments were moving in that direction.

---

[1] http://en.wikipedia.org/wiki/Samuel_Taylor_Coleridge
[2] http://en.wikipedia.org/wiki/The_Rime_of_the_Ancient_Mariner
[3] http://www.economicnoise.com/?p=49174
[4] http://www.economicnoise.com/?p=48944

44.2 Key Indicators

Two key indicators to determine whether impeachment probabilities are increasing or decreasing pertain to the Democrat Party and the media. One or both must abandon Obama before impeachment is possible.

Impeachment is a political process more than a legal one. It has standing in the Constitution, but should only be invoked rarely and under the right political circumstances.

Neither the Democrat Party nor the media is on board for impeachment. Both continue to support Barack Obama, at least superficially. He is no longer the newcomer-king upon whom adulation and praise was undeservedly poured. Much of the public no longer supports him or his policies. That puts Democrat and media supporters in an uncomfortable position.

Nothing that Obama has done can be called an achievement, at least a positive one. The medical system is in disarray and additional unpleasant surprises will continue as ObamaCare rolls out. The economy is not recovering. Joblessness (the real number) is a disgrace. Our allies are embarrassed by US foreign policy blunders and slights. Obama's penchant for lying is now widely recognized. He is up to his neck in scandals.

In short, Obama has fallen from savior to our worst president in just five years.

Both Democrats and media invested heavily in this newcomer and it will not be easy for either to disengage. The saga of Barack Obama has not worn well. Both groups are cognizant of that and assessing their personal exposure. Continuing to defend him may represent an existential threat. If so, they will abandon him.

The most overt and ominous sign is provided by Democrats up for re-election. None want to be seen with Obama. He has leper-like appeal as a result of his policies and declining poll numbers.

That was before the brouhaha raised over the latest Benghazi memo. Reaction to that has just begun but will likely create more distance between him and his supporters.

The Democrat Party loved their messiah. Now that he has fallen, they behave like Peter from the Gospels – "Obama? I don't believe I know the gentleman."

It would be nice to say that a sense of integrity, ethics or concern for the American citizens motivated their unease. Sadly, it is nothing more than the survival instinct surfacing. It is an instinct that all forms of life, including the lowest and crudest, have in common.

The media (up to now an unofficial wing of the Democrat Party) has become cautious. Several have distanced themselves, seemingly embarrassed about how they were taken in by this mountebank.

The media fell for the man and were instrumental in creating the myth that allowed him to defeat Hillary in the primaries and then two Republicans in elections. Whether they knew he was a phony or not when they promoted him is irrelevant. The fact that the public now sees his lack of substance and competence creates the threat for them.

Neither media nor Democrats have switched allegiances yet. Perhaps they never will. However, their support is not as enthusiastic. It is tempered by concerns regarding their own future.

Carefully crafted distancing occurs in the event full abandonment becomes necessary. The impenetrable armor that once shielded Obama is beginning to look more like paper mache. The media are loathe to attack him, but show less inclination to cover for him.

The media position will continue to remain cautious unless the Democrats turn on Obama. That turning, may already be underway. James Freeman reports in the WSJ[5]:

---

[5]http://online.wsj.com/news/articles/SB10001424052702304431104579549463617452496?mod=djemMER_h&mg=reno64-wsj&url=http%3A%2F%2Fonline.wsj.com%2Farticle%2FSB10001424052702304431104579549463617452496.html%3Fmod%3DdjemMER_h

"President Obama and his aides may view IRS targeting as one of Washington's "phony scandals," but more than two dozen House Democrats now officially disagree. On Wednesday, 26 Members from the President's party joined with Republicans in voting to urge Attorney General Eric Holder[6] "to appoint a special counsel to investigate the targeting of conservative nonprofit groups by the Internal Revenue Service." And no, these Democrats aren't all lonely moderates representing conservative districts in deep-red states. Among the Democrats backing a special prosecutor are Representatives from California, Connecticut, Hawaii, Massachusetts and New York."

44.3 The Democrats

Democrats had a meal ticket they rode to victory (except for the last mid-term election which was historic in terms of their defeat). Their thoroughbred now looks more like an old, worn-out, plow horse. Obama has become an albatross. They still shoot horses I suppose, but what do they do with albatrosses? We may see over the next couple of years.

Mr. Freeman's observation is not unexpected in the amoral world of politics. No matter how good or bad your guy, **you support him if the benefits of doing so exceed the costs of doing so.** That calculus describes **the entirety of political loyalty and integrity.**

That calculus is now looking shaky for Obama. His star power is almost gone and that was realistically all that he had. A crossover point where costs exceed benefits is near. Should that happen, Obama is **figuratively worth more dead than alive.** When Obama threatens the future of individual Democrats or the party itself, that crossover point has been passed.

---

[6]http://topics.wsj.com/person/H/Eric-Holder/6924

44.4 The Media

If the Democrats wobble, the media will wobble with them. The media cannot support someone if he becomes an outcast in his own party. Ideology aside, the media have families to feed just like the rest of us.

The media is frustrated (fed up?) with Jay Carney and clearly show that. Press conferences, once love-fests, are now highly contentious. The media cannot afford to continue to look like toadies given Obama's drop in popularity and potential problems.

Democrats and the media now treat Barack Obama as if he were radioactive and they don't have the knowledge as to how to properly handle this material. The effusive worship is gone and will never return.

Both groups are walking on egg shells (albatross eggs?). They know that taking the wrong side in this evolving situation could be career-ending. **Come out against Obama too early and the Democrat machine will end their careers. Support him too long and voters/readers may end their careers.**

Media and Democrat politicians are caught in the middle of a dangerous and evolving situation. Theirs is a fascinating balancing act to watch. One misstep could be career-ending.

Which way this drama tilts will be determined by further revelations pertaining to the Obama scandals. Key political and media players must be agile and adjust to these and the public's reaction.

Republicans are not exempt from risks. They could snatch defeat from the apparent jaws of victory by overplaying their hand.

Conditions for impeachment are not here yet, but the process underway seems to have a momentum that suggests they are coming. Supporters seem increasingly unwilling to sacrifice themselves in order to protect the president.

Albatrosses are not endangered species in politics. They are always considered nuisances, always in season and always eliminated.

45 Ripple or Tidal Wave?

MAY 13, 2014

It is too early to make predictions of a tidal wave election for 2014. (Even a week or a day out may be too soon, based on my last attempt.)

Obama's future may be directly tied to this election. Under the best of circumstances, Obama's effectiveness is over. To put that into perspective, think about what Obama accomplished in his first five plus years. He rammed ObamaCare through and that was the end of legislative achievements. That is not to say that harm was not done via other channels.

The passage of ObamaCare prematurely doomed Obama's presidency. A tidal wave in the up-coming mid-terms could literally end his presidency. Such a result would also threaten the Democrat Party as a viable force in American politics.

In Obama's case, a tidal wave election could lead to impeachment. It is probably a necessary but not sufficient condition. There would also have to be stronger evidence of lawbreaking or malfeasance. Given the number of potential skeletons in scandal closets, a willingness to force some doors open would likely provide this evidence.

Democrats who survive a negative wave election may be averse to defending the man who will be deemed responsible. A wave election might also determine whether Hillary Clinton runs in 2016. My guess is that she won't, even if 2014 doesn't turn out to as disastrous as the numbers today suggest. But that's another story for another day.

Larry Sabato has spent his life handicapping elections (it should be noted that he called the 2012 presidential election incorrectly).

His possible outcomes at this point cover a wide range of scenarios. The table below was reported by Rick Moran[1], based on Sabato's assessments:

Scenario	Potential R pickups		Outcome D*	Outcome R	Current Chances
Beach week	None; Ds add GA or KY	+1	56	44	A minuscule notch above zero
Calm Seas: Democrats stay even	No seats change hands		55	45	Tiny
Ripple: Two open Democratic seats switch	SD, WV	+2	53	47	Minimal
Small Breakers: Four Democratic seats switch	AR, MT, SD, WV	+4	51	49	Possible with around 50% Obama job approval and/or enough GOP gaffes
Sea Wall Holds: Democrats keep majority with Biden tie-breaker	AR, MT, LA, SD, WV	+5	50	50	Probable if Obama stabilizes and GOP makes an error or two
Sea Wall Breached: GOP wins six of seven Democratic Senate seats in Romney states	AK, AR, MT, LA, SD, WV	+6	49	51	Slightly probable at present
Gale Force White Caps: GOP sweeps all Romney states	AK, AR, LA, MT, NC, SD, WV	+7	48	52	Credible outcome with modest GOP surge in fall
Tropical Storm Wave: GOP grabs two seats in Democratic-leaning states	AK, AR, CO, IA, LA, MT, NC, SD, WV	+9	46	54	Likely best plausible Republican result— GOP surges, Obama falls
Republican Tidal Wave: GOP secures four seats in Democratic-leaning states (CO, IA, MI, NH)	AK, AR, CO, IA, LA, MI, MT, NC, NH, SD, WV	+11	44	56	Outside chance, not inconceivable with enough Obama stumbles and GOP breaks
Full GOP Tsunami: GOP nominees even win Democratic seats once thought safe (MN, OR, VA)	AK, AR, CO, IA, LA, MI, MN, MT, NC, NH, OR, SD, VA, WV	+14	41	59	Very unlikely at present; requires near-total Obama collapse and poor Democratic campaigns

Table I

Mr. Moran added:

"According to the chart, much will depend on President Obama's approval ratings come November. Rich

---

[1]http://www.americanthinker.com/blog/2014/05/sabato_how_big_a_gop_wave.html

Baehr and others don't see the president's numbers recovering very much given what's ahead with more Obamacare surprises and a still moribund economy."

It is difficult to disagree with Moran's assessment. If it is correct, we could have political fireworks ahead.

46 Is The Country Too Far Gone?

In terms of rescuing the country, that may be the case. That conclusion is nearly independent to what happens with or to Barack Obama.

A century of political attacks on the the Constitution has emasculated this essential constraint on government. Little now stands between the citizen and the predatory State. History knows no example of governments willingly relinquishing power. The United States will not be an exception.

President Obama did not create the Constitutional issues, although he exploited them and advanced them. Whether he goes or stays in office has little to do with reining in the State. That problem is independent of Obama and ultimately bigger and more difficult to solve.

Removing Obama does nothing to reverse the course of the country. Someone just as bad and likely worse will eventually occupy the office. Why the worst rise to the top was explained by Friedrich Hayek in his "Road to Serfdom."

It took Rome hundreds of years to fall. It will not take that long for the United States.

The country is at a tipping point that was inevitable with or without Barack Obama. It is a point that all great civilizations reach. None before have dealt with it well. The US will be no different unless the principles of the Constitution can be restored and government put back into its cage.